From .... German .... *Department*

THE UNIVERSITY OF KANSAS
LAWRENCE, KANSAS 66045

Gary Roy

Für besondere Leistungen im Deutschen

1991-1992

Awards Committee

5-83-30M

Austria in Poetry and History

Anthology of Austrian Literature

Volume I: Poetry

Austria in Poetry and History

Bilingual

Selected and introduced by
FREDERICK UNGAR

English translations by
LOWELL A. BANGERTER et al.

Frederick Ungar Publishing Co. / New York

Library of Congress Cataloging in Publication Data
Main entry under title:

Austria in poetry and history.

(Anthology of Austrian literature; v. 1)
Text in English and German.
Includes index.
 1. Austrian poetry (German)—Translations into English.
2. German poetry—Austrian authors—Translations into
English. 3. English poetry—Translations from German.
4. Austrian poetry (German) 5. German poetry—Austrian
authors. 6. Austria—History—Poetry. I. Ungar,
Frederick. II. Series.
PT3824.Z5A75 1984   831'.008'09436   83-24152
ISBN 0-8044-2941-3

Copyright © 1984 by
Frederick Ungar Publishing Co., Inc.
Printed in the United States of America

Die Dichter sind überall, schon ihrem Begriff nach, die Bewahrer der Natur. Wo sie dieses nicht mehr ganz sein können ... da werden sie als die Zeugen und als die Rächer der Natur auftreten.
—Friedrich Schiller
Über naive und sentimentalische Dichtung

Poets are everywhere, by the very concept, preservers of nature. Where they can no longer be that completely, ... they appear as witnesses and avengers of nature.
—Friedrich Schiller
Naive and Sentimental Poetry

EINLEITUNG

Wie der Titel der vorliegenden Sammlung anzeigt, liegt der Nachdruck auf Perioden und Ereignissen österreichischer Geschichte. Chronologisch angeordnet, obwohl mehrfach von Themengruppen anderer Art unterbrochen, beginnt sie mit den ersten dichterischen Zeugnissen, denen der Minnesänger des zwölften und dreizehnten Jahrhunderts. Die folgenden Jahrhunderte bieten wenig von dichterischem Wert oder von dem, was heute noch genießbar gefunden würde, und erst vom frühen neunzehnten Jahrhundert an gibt es eine Reihe namhafter Gedichte.

Österreichische Geschichte im Gedicht setzt erst mit dem ersten Weltkrieg ein. Auf anfängliche patriotische Kriegsbegeisterung folgt bald Ernüchterung und dann Protest, der in leidenschaftlichen Versen Ausdruck findet. Die Folgen des verlorenen Krieges, der Zusammenbruch der Monarchie, Elend, Entbehrung und Hoffnungslosigkeit sind im Gedicht lebensvoll dargestellt. Wir erleben im Gedicht die Zeit der Vaterländischen Front, die in der Beschießung des Karl-Marx Hofs ihren unheilvollen Höhepunkt findet. Ebenso die Besetzung Österreichs durch Hitler-Deutschland, die Auswanderung oder Flucht der Gefährdeten, ihre Leiden und jene der in ihrer Heimat Verbliebenen. Empörung und Klage über die Menschenopfer in den Konzentrations- und Vernichtungslagern finden im Einklang mit dem Motto dieses Buches dichterischen Ausdruck. Ebenso die Schicksale der Auswanderer und ihre ambivalenten Gefühle gegenüber ihrer früheren Heimat. Der Zusammenbruch Deutschlands, mit dramatischer Wucht dargestellt, ist das letzte geschichtbezogene Gedicht. Österreichs Selbstbesinnung und ein hoffnungsvoller Ausblick in eine lichtere Zukunft beschließen die Sammlung.

Es erfüllt mich mit Genugtuung, daß ich in ihr eine Anzahl von

Gedichten aufnehmen konnte, die ich seinerzeit im Saturn Verlag, Wien veröffentlichte, nämlich in *Österreichs Lyrik der Gegenwart* (1930) und in *Das Herz Europas. Ein österreichisches Vortragsbuch* (1933).

Es mag auch am Platze sein, einiges über die hier gebotenen Übersetzungen zu sagen, sowie über Übersetzungen im Allgemeinen. Sie werden in der Regel abschätzig beurteilt. Man bemängelt an ihnen, daß sie dem Original nicht gerecht werden und daß daher manches von seiner Wirkung verloren geht. Zwar ist es richtig, daß viel von der magischen Wirkung eines großen Gedichts eingebüßt wird, wenn nicht der Kunst des Übersetzers auch die Gunst der Sprache seiner Bemühung zur Hilfe kommt. Ist nun die Frage, ob ein teilweiser Verlust dem des ganzen—alles Übersetzen abzuschwören und in völliger Unkenntnis fremdsprachiger Dichtung zu verbleiben—vorzuziehen ist, nicht leicht zu entscheiden. Soll man, wenn Vollkommenes nicht zu erreichen ist darauf verzichten, das Erreichbare anzustreben? Die allzu strengen Kritiker einer Übersetzung würden milder gestimmt sein, wenn sie sich die enorme Schwierigkeit einer solchen vergegenwärtigen wollten, die darin besteht, Sinn, Versmaß und Reim beizubehalten und mit ihnen die Reinheit der Sprache, die dramatische Spannung und die dem Original innewohnende Magik.

Es kommt hinzu, daß die Unmöglichkeit einer kongenialen Übersetzung von den Vertretern dieser Denkrichtung oft an sehr schwachen Übersetzungen zu beweisen versucht wird. Dem gegenüber kann auf vorzügliche Übersetzungen hingewiesen werden, wie es hier durch die Aufnahme einiger solcher von englischen Gedichten ins Deutsche unter Beweis gestellt ist. Sie dürfen als eigenständige Dichtungen gewertet werden.

Lyrik der letzten Jahrzehnte ist hier nur spärlich vertreten, die der beiden allerletzten gar nicht, und zwar deshalb weil mir bedeutende oder auf österreichische Geschichte bezogene Gedichte aus diesen Jahren trotz sorgfältiger Nachforschung, auch solcher die mit Hilfe von Wiener Freunden unternommen wurden, nicht bekannt geworden sind. Es ist dennoch wahrscheinlich und gewiß zu hoffen, daß auch in diesen Jahren gute Gedichte geschrieben wurden und eben nur unveröffentlicht geblieben sind.

All dies gibt mir die willkommene Gelegenheit, mich mit der zeitgenössischen Dichtung auseinanderzusetzen. Wenn unter dem traditionellem Begriff "Dichtung" die höchste sprachliche Kunstform verstanden ist, in der Sinnfülle mit Wohlklang zu unauflöslicher Einheit verschmelzen, dann sind experimentelle Dichtung und ähnliche Abweichungen von der Tradition auszuschließen. In der neuesten Lyrik löst sich oft alle Form auf. Der Vers wird zu einer willkürlich abgeteilten Prosa, die so ein Chaos von Silben und Satzbruchstücken bildet. Auf diese Weise bleibt das Gedicht durch seine offenbar beabsichtigte Dunkelheit Nichteingeweihten verschlossen. Nicht selten wird auch ein Gedicht in einem Druckbild angeboten, das es nur durch dieses von Prosa unterscheidet. Ein ander Mal erweckt es den Anschein, als ob der Dichter nur zu sich selbst spräche und keinen Wert darauf läge, vom Leser verstanden zu werden. Dieser neuartige Zustand der Künste ist, wie bekannt, keineswegs auf Österreich oder auf Dichtung beschränkt. Aber es stellt das Überleben von Dichtung selbst in Frage.

Die vorliegende Sammlung ist, wie eingangs erwähnt, nicht repräsentativ in dem Sinne, daß sie alle Richtungen österreichischer Lyrik bietet. Obwohl sie von einem speziellen Gesichtspunkt ausgeht, repräsentiert sie dennoch österreichische Dichtung in einem ihrer, wie ich glaube, nicht unwürdigem Sinn. Und so möge sie als bescheidener Versuch aufgenommen werden, der Dichtung in ihrem hergebrachten Sinn zu dienen.

FREDERICK UNGAR

INTRODUCTION

As expressed in the title, the emphasis of this collection is on periods and events of Austrian history. Arranged chronologically—although interrupted by groups of various themes—the book starts with the earliest poetic testimonies, that of the minstrels of the twelfth and thirteenth centuries. The centuries that followed offer little of poetic value, little that would be found enjoyable today. Only as late as the early nineteenth century are there a number of notable poems.

Austrian history in fine poetry is found no earlier than in our century, which unfortunately has provided us with more history than we bargained for. Such poetry begins with the First World War. Initial patriotic war enthusiasm was soon followed by disillusionment and thereafter protest passionately expressed in poems. The consequences of the lost war, the collapse of the monarchy, misery, deprivation, and hopelessness are vividly captured. In poetry we live through the years of the "Patriotic Front" and their fateful climax in the bombardment of the "Karl Marx Hof." Presented also are the occupation of Austria by Hitler's Germany, the emigration or flight of those in danger, their suffering and that of those who remained behind. Deeply felt indignation and lament over the victims in the concentration and liquidation camps, reflecting the motto of the present volume, find expression in poems of high emotion. There is also a reminder of the fate of the emigrants and their ambivalent feelings toward their native land. The collapse of Germany, expressed with dramatic power, is the last history-related poem. Austria's self-contemplation and a more hopeful outlook for a brighter future conclude the collection.

It is with satisfaction that I could include in the present collection a number of poems that I published in Saturn Verlag, Wien, in *Österreichs Lyrik der Gegenwart* (1930) and in *Das Herz Europas, Ein österreichisches Vortragsbuch* (1933).

It may also be in order to say a few words about the translations offered here, and about translations in general. They are often judged disparagingly because they do not do full justice to the original poem and lose much of its poetic effect. Admittedly, much of the magical impact of great poetry is often dissipated if the translator's effort is not bolstered by favorable language and his own skill. But is it not preferable to accept a partial loss of the effect of great poetry rather than abjure translation altogether and thus remain in total ignorance of foreign-language poetry? The all too severe critics of translations would be less severe in judgment if they realized the enormous difficulty of the task (which calls for fully maintaining meaning, meter, and rhyme, and simultaneously the purity of language, dramatic tension, and the magic of the original). Further, people of this persuasion try to prove the impossibility of congenial translations often by using poor translations as examples. Against this view, excellent translations can be summoned up, among them, such as are included in this volume, particularly English poems in German versions. They may be evaluated as great poems in their own right.

Poetry of the last decades is only scantily represented here, and that of the last two decades not at all. Despite careful research, with the help of Viennese friends, I could not find any worthwhile poems of these years, or any related to Austrian history. Nevertheless, it is quite likely and certainly to be hoped that also in these years good poems have been written, but just have remained unpublished.

All this gives me a welcome opportunity to take issue with contemporary poetry. If the traditional concept of poetry defines the highest art form using words, in which profundity of meaning is fused with melodiousness into indissoluble unity, then experimental poetry and similar deviations from tradition are automatically excluded. Because in much contemporary poetry all form is dissolved, verse is often an arbitrarily divided prose, which in turn forms a chaos of syllables and sentence fractions. The poem, then, because of its apparently intended obscurity, remains closed to the uninitiated. Such poetry frequently differs from prose only in its typographical presentation. At other times the poet, it seems, speaks to himself and does not care to be understood by his readers.

This novel condition of the arts is, of course, not restricted to

Austria or to poetry. But it puts the survival of poetry itself, as it has been understood, in jeopardy.

The present collection, as stated above, is not representative of Austrian poetry in the sense that it includes all its variations. Although its emphasis is on a special viewpoint, I believe it nevertheless represents Austrian poetry in a way not unworthy of it. May this volume, then, be received as a modest attempt to serve poetry in its traditional sense.

FREDERICK UNGAR

Austria or to poetry. But it puts the survival of poetry itself, as it has been understood, in jeopardy.

The present collection, as stated above, is not representative of Austrian poetry in the sense that it includes all its variations. Although its emphasis is on a special viewpoint, I believe it nevertheless represents Austrian poetry in a way not unworthy of it. May this volume, then, be received as a modest attempt to serve poetry in its traditional sense.

FREDERICK UNGAR

CONTENTS

Einleitung		vii
Introduction		xi
Der von Kürenberg	Ich zog mir einen Falken	2
	I Raised Myself a Falcon	3
Dietmar von Aist	Es stand eine Frau alleine	4
	A Lady Stood Alone	5
Walther von der Vogelweide	Unter der Linde	6
	Under the Linden	7
	O weh! wohin entschwanden...	8
	Alas! Where Have They Vanished, All Those Years of Mine!	9
	Ich saß auf einem Steine	10
	I Sat upon a Stone	11
Abraham a Santa Clara	Der Mond	12
	The Moon	13
Catharina Regina von Greiffenberg	Auf die fröhlich und herrliche Auferstehung Christi	14
	Concerning the Joyous and Splendid Resurrection of Christ	15
	Gott lobende Frühlingslust	14
	Spring-Joy Praising God	15
	Das beglückende Unglück	16
	Fortune-bringing Misfortune	17
Laurentius von Schnüffis	Lobet ihr Himmel den Höchsten dort oben	18
	Praise, oh You Heavens, the Highest on High	19
Martin Joseph Pradstetter	An Kloen	22
	To Chloe	23

Pradstetter *cont'd*	Danklied	22
	Song of Thanks	23
Marianne von Willemer	An den Westwind	26
	To the West Wind	27
Anonym	Prinz Eugen	28
	Prince Eugene	29
Anonym	O, du lieber Augustin	30
	O You Jolly Augustine	31
Ferdinand Raimund	Brüderlein fein	32
	My Brother Dear	33
	Lied des Valentin	34
	Valentin's Song	35
	Abschied	36
	Farewell	37
Hermann von Gilm	Allerseelen	38
	All Souls' Day	39
	Die Nacht	38
	Night	39
	Ein Grab	40
	A Grave	41
Marie von Ebner-Eschenbach	Ein kleines Lied	42
	A Little Song	43
	Grabschrift	42
	Epitaph	43
Nikolaus Lenau	Der Postillion	44
	The Postillion	45
	Bitte	48
	Prayer	49
	Die Drei	48
	The Three	49
	Die drei Zigeuner	50
	The Three Gypsies	51
Adalbert Stifter	Herbstabend	54
	Autumn Evening	55
Anastasius Grün	Im Winter	56
	In Winter	57
Ferdinand von Saar	Schlummerlied	58
	Lullaby	59
	Herbst	58
	Fall	59
	Wieder!	60

	Again!	61
	Alter	60
	Age	61
	Landschaft im Spätherbst	62
	Landscape in Late Autumn	63
Josef Mohr	Weihnachtslied	64
	Christmas Song	65
Franz Grillparzer	Zwischen Gaeta und Kapua	66
	Between Gaeta and Capua	67
Richard von Schaukal	Vorfrühling	68
	Early Spring	69
	An den Herrn	70
	To the Lord	71
Richard Beer-Hofmann	Schlaflied für Mirjam	72
	Lullaby for Mirjam	73
	Altern	74
	Aging	75
Arthur Schnitzler	Sprüche in Versen	78
	Sayings in Verse	79
Ernst Goll	Königszug	82
	Royal Procession	83
	Herbstliche Fülle	84
	Autumn Fullness	85
	Blüten	86
	Blossoms	87
Richard Billinger	Wir Bauern	88
	We Peasants	89
	Die Soldatenbraut	90
	The Soldier's Betrothed	91
Max Fleischer	Reiche Ernte	92
	Rich Harvest	93
Anton Wildgans	Ich bin ein Kind der Stadt	94
	I Am a City Child	95
	Akkord	96
	Chord	97
	Letzte Erkenntnis	98
	Final Knowledge	99
Max Mell	Heimat	100
	Homeland	101
Felix Braun	Wie lange—?	102
	How long?	103

Alfred Margul-Sperber	Der Tag der Landschaft	104
	The Day of the Landscape	105
Paula Ludwig	Jahresneige	106
	End of the Year	107
Herta Felicia Staub	September	110
	September	111
Christine Busta	Mein Geliebter . . .	112
	My Beloved . . .	113
	Dem lieben Gott	114
	To the Dear Lord	115
Ingeborg Bachmann	Die große Fracht	116
	The Great Freight	117
Georg Trakl	Verklärter Herbst	118
	Effulgent Autumn	119
	Ein Winterabend	118
	A Winter Evening	119
	Der Herbst der Einsamen	120
	Autumn of the Lonely	121
Hugo von Hofmannsthal	Vorfrühling	122
	Early Spring	123
	Die Beiden	124
	The Two	125
	Über Vergänglichkeit	124
	On Transitoriness	125
	Prolog zu dem Buch "Anatol"	126
	Prologue to the Book "Anatol"	127
Rainer Maria Rilke	Herbsttag	132
	Autumn Day	133
	Der Panther	132
	The Panther	133
Karl Kraus	Unter dem Wasserfall	134
	Under the Waterfall	135
	Vor einem Springbrunnen	136
	Before a Fountain	137
Carl Dallago	Sommerstrophen	140
	Summer Stanzas	141
Ludwig Goldscheider	Monatsverse	142
	Month-Verses	143
	Sommernacht	146

	Summer Night	147
	Gespräch mit dem Mond	150
	Conversation with the Moon	151
Ida Schwarz	An eine Wolke	152
	To a Cloud	153
Otto Stoessl	Mondfabel	154
	Moon Fable	155
Josef Weinheber	Im Grase	156
	In the Grass	157
Arthur Zanker	Hochzeitssonett	158
	Wedding Sonnet	159
	Großelternhaus	160
	Grandparents' House	161
Joseph Georg Oberkofler	Der Erbe	162
	The Heir	163
Alma Johanna Koenig	Traurige Ode	164
	Sad Ode	165
	Credo	166
	What I Believe	167
Eugenie Fink	Lebensdank	168
	Gratitude to Life	169
Herbert Strutz	Märznacht	170
	March Night	171
	Ein Bauernsohn schreibt aus der Stadt	172
	A Farmer's Son Writes from the City	173
Hans Leifhelm	Winterwald	174
	Winter Forest	175
	Herbstlicher Ruf	174
	Autumn Call	175
	Lob der Vergänglichkeit	176
	Praise of Transitoriness	177
	Vom hoffenden Leben	178
	On the Hoping Life	179
Franz Grillparzer	Lob Österreichs	182
	In Praise of Austria	183
Anton Wildgans	Österreichisches Lied	184
	Austrian Song	185
Paula von Preradović	Land der Berge, Land am Strome	186

Preradović *cont'd*	Land of Mountains, Riverland	187
Ferdinand von Saar	Zweite Wiener Elegie	188
	Second Viennese Elegy	189
Hans Just	Nächtlicher Gang durch die Burg	190
	Night Walk through the Burg	191
Emmy Klein-Synek	Wien im Frühling	194
	Vienna in Spring	195
Martina Wied	Sankt Stephan	196
	Saint Stephen's	197
Erika Mitterer	Stadtpark	198
	City Park	199
Friedrich Torberg	Prater Hauptallee	200
	Prater's Tree-lined Boulevard	201
	Blick vom Kobenzl	202
	View from the Kobenzl	203
Josef Weinheber	Alt-Ottakring	204
	Old Ottakring	205
	Liebhartstal	206
	Liebhartstal	207
Alma Johanna Koenig	Waldviertel. Niederösterreich	208
	Waldviertel. Lower Austria	209
Paula von Preradović	Oberösterreichische Landschaft	210
	Upper-Austrian Landscape	211
Martha Hoffmann	Alt-Aussee	212
	Old Aussee	213
Lilly Sauter	Vollmond in Salzburg	214
	Full Moon in Salzburg	215
Natalie Beer	Mein Vorarlberg	216
	My Vorarlberg	217
Herbert Strutz	Gnade der Heimat (Kärnten)	218
	Grace of the Homeland (Carinthia)	219

Hans Kloepfer	Spätherbst in der Steiermark	220
	Late Autumn in Styria	221
Mida Huber	Heimatlied (Burgenland)	222
	Song of Home (Burgenland)	223
Ernst Waldinger	Musik für diese Zeit	224
	Music for this Time	225
Eugenie Fink	Mozart	228
	Mozart	229
Ernst Waldinger	Mozart, Klavierkonzert Nr. 20 in D-Moll, KV 466	230
	Mozart, Piano Concerto No. 20, in D Minor	231
	"Auch ist das klopfende Herz schon angezeigt"	230
	"Even the Beating Heart Is Already Indicated"	231
	Beethovensonate	232
	Beethoven Sonata	233
Michael Klieba	Schubert	234
	Schubert	235
Friedrich Halm	Mein Herz, ich will dich fragen	236
	My Heart, I Want to Ask You	237
Nikolaus Lenau	An die Entfernte	238
	To Her Far Away	239
Karl Kraus	Verwandlung	240
	Transformation	241
	Auferstehung	240
	Resurrection	241
Hans Leifhelm	Mit dem Sichelmond, mit dem Abendstern	242
	With the Crescent Moon, with the Evening Star	243
Alexander Lernet-Holenia	Asokas Liebeslied	246
	Asoka's Love Song	247
Lilly Sauter	Sehnsucht	248

Sauter *cont'd*	Longing	249
Christina Busta	Jahreszeiten	250
	Seasons	251
Herbert Strutz	Mädchen im Frühling	252
	Maidens in Spring	253
Otto Stoessl	Liebe	254
	Love	255
Hugo Zuckermann	Reiterlied	256
	Cavalry Song	257
Josef Luitpold	Trotziger Abschied	258
	Defiant Farewell	259
Karl Kraus	Der sterbende Soldat	260
	The Dying Soldier	261
	Volkshymne	260
	National Folk Hymn	261
	Silvester 1917	264
	New Year's Eve 1917	265
	Flieder	264
	Lilacs	265
	Zum ewigen Frieden	266
	Toward Eternal Peace	267
Franz Theodor Csokor	Heimkehr 1918	270
	Homecoming 1918	271
Berthold Viertel	Der Februar	272
	February	273
	Auswanderer	274
	Emigrants	275
	Die deutsche Sprache	276
	The German Language	277
Helene Kafka (Ordensname Restituta)	Soldatenlied	278
	Soldier's Song	279
Hans Just	Weihnachten	282
	Christmas	283
	Der Mond	282
	The Moon	283
Jura Soyfer	Dachau-Lied	284
	Song of the Austrians in Dachau	285

Käthe Leichter	An meine Brüder	288
	To My Brothers	289
Paula von Preradović	Wiener Reimchronik	292
	Chronicle in Verse	293
	Der Abstand	292
	Perspective	293
	Fliegeralarm	292
	Air Raid Alarm	293
	Luftangriff	294
	Air Raid	295
	Frauengefängnis der Gestapo	296
	Women's Prison of the Gestapo	297
	Schlacht	298
	Battle	299
	Der Dom	298
	The Cathedral	299
Theodor Kramer	Der Ofen von Lublin	302
	The Oven of Lublin	303
Ilse Weber	Weg nach Theresienstadt	304
	The Road to Terezin	305
Paul Celan	Todesfuge	306
	Death Fugue	307
Ernst Waldinger	Der falsche Prophet	310
	The False Prophet	311
	Sie haben unser Heimweh getötet!	312
	They Have Killed Our Longing for Our Homeland	313
	Von der Liebe zur Heimat	312
	On Love of the Homeland	313
	Verzeihen, aber nicht vergessen	314
	Forgive, but Do Not Forget	315
	Die Mahnmale	316
	The Memorials	317
	Papst Johannes XXIII	316
	Pope John XXIII	317
	Ich bin ein Sohn der deutschen Sprache	318

Waldinger *cont'd*	I Am a Son of the German Language	319
	Bericht aus Deutschland, 1944	320
	Report from Germany, 1944	321
Gertrud Fussenegger	Wie weit	322
	How Far	323
Erika Mitterer	An Österreich	326
	To Austria	327
Emmy Klein-Synek	Du neues Jahr	330
	You New Year	331

Translations into German

William Wordsworth	Composed upon Westminster Bridge	332
Ludwig Goldscheider	An der Westminster Brücke	333
William Wordsworth	The Universe—A Shell	334
Ludwig Goldscheider	Das All eine Muschel	335
Joyce Kilmer	Trees	336
Ernst Waldinger	Bäume	337
George Santayana	O World!	338
Ernst Waldinger	O Welt!	339

Middle High German texts

Der von Kürenberg	Ich zog mir einen Falken	340
Dietmar von Aist	Es stand ein Frau alleine	340
Walther von der Vogelweide	Unter der Linde	341
	O weh! wohin entschwand	342
	Ich saß auf einem Steine	342

Copyright Acknowledgments	344
Index by Translator	345

DER VON KÜRENBERG

ICH ZOG MIR EINEN FALKEN*

Ich zog mir einen Falken   für mehr als ein Jahr.
Als ich ihn gezähmt   wie ich ihn haben wollte,
und ich ihm sein Gefieder   mit vielem Gold umwand,
da hob er sich zu großer Höhe   und flog in andere Land.

Seitdem sah ich den Falken   schön dahin fliegen:
er führte an seinem Fuße   seidene Riemen,
und war all sein Gefieder   rötlich gold.
Gott führe sie zusammen   die gerne geliebt wollen sein!

*The Middle High German text is on p. 340

I RAISED MYSELF A FALCON

I raised myself a falcon   trained him more than a year.
When I had him broken in   as I would have him be,
And I had wound his feathers well   with gold, a shining band,
He rose up very high then   and flew to another land.

I've since seen the falcon   flying grandly:
He carried upon his foot then   fine silken jesses,
And too his handsome plumage was   all reddish gold.
May God e'er them together bring   who love each other so dearly!

DIETMAR VON AIST

ES STAND EINE FRAU ALLEINE*

Es stand eine Frau alleine
Und harrte über die Heide,
Und harrte ihres Liebsten.
Da sah sie Falken fliegen.
„O wohl dir, Falke, wie du bist!
Du fliegst, wohin dir lieb ist:
Du wähltest dir im Walde
Einen Baum, der dir gefalle.
Also hab auch ich getan:
Ich erkor mir selber einen Mann,
Den erwählten meine Augen.
Das neiden schöne Frauen.
O weh, was lassen sie nicht mein Lieb?
Ich begehrte keinen ihrer Trauten je."

*The Middle High German text is on p. 340

A LADY STOOD ALONE

Alone a lady was standing
and looking o'er the heather,
and looking for her lover,
when she saw there falcons flying.
"O falcon, fortunate are you!
You fly where'er you want to:
For yourself you choose in the forest
one tree that you find pleasing.
Likewise have I also done:
I have chosen for myself a man,
my own eyes have him selected.
Fair ladies now are jealous.
O when will they leave me my love?
After all, I never desired to take their men."

WALTHER VON DER VOGELWEIDE

UNTER DER LINDE*

Unter der Linde
an der Heide
wo unser zweier Bette war,
da möget ihr finden
gebrochen beide
Blumen und Gras.
Vor dem Walde in einem Tal
tandaradei!
   schön sang da die Nachtigall.

Ich kam gegangen
zu der Aue:
dahin war mein Schatz gekommen schon.
Da ward ich empfangen:
hehre Frau,
das macht mich selig für immerdar.
Küßte er mich? wohl tausendmal!
tandaradei!
   seht wie rot mir ist der Mund.

Dort hatte er gemacht,
ach so herrlich
von Blumen eine Bettstelle.
Darüber wird noch lachen
verständnisinnig
wenn jemand kommt des Wegs vorbei
Bei den Rosen, er mag wohl,
tandaradei!
   merken wo das Haupt mir lag.

---

*The Middle High German text is on p. 341

UNDER THE LINDEN

Under the linden,
mid the heather,
there where we two had our bed,
there you will find them,
neat together,
the grass and broken blossoms wed.
Near the forest, down in a vale,
tandaradei,
    lovely sang the nightingale.

I came a-walking
to the meadow,
there had my love arrived before,
there was I addressed as
"Noble Lady,"
'Twill make me happy evermore.
Kissed he me? A thousandfold!
Tandaradei!
    Now how red my lips, behold!

There for us he'd made,
richly piling
the blossoms fresh, a lovely bed.
Where the blooms were laid
there'll be smiling,
if someone o'er that path is led.
In the roses he well may,
tandaradei,
    espy where my head had lain.

Daß er bei mir lag,
wüßte es jemand
(was Gott verhüte!), so schämte ich mich.
Was er mit mir getan hat,
nimmer und niemand
soll je das wissen, nur er und ich
und ein kleines Vögelein,
tandaradei!
das wird wohl verschwiegen sein.

O WEH! WOHIN ENTSCHWANDEN...*

O weh! wohin entschwanden
War nur ein Traum mein Leben
Was mir stets wirklich deuchte,
Ich habe lang geschlafen,
Nun bin ich aufgewacht
was mir so kund einst war
Land und Leute alle
sind mir so fremd geworden
Die mir Gespielen waren
Umbrochen ist das Feld,
Wenn nicht das Wasser flöße
fürwahr ich müßte meinen
Mich grüßet mancher träge
Die Welt fiel allenthalben
Wenn ich gedenke heute
der mir nun ist zerronnen
Für immerdar, o weh.

alle meine Jahr?
oder ist es wahr?
war's ein trüglich Spiel?
so daß es mir entfiel.
und mir ist unbekannt
wie diese meine Hand.
die meine Kinderjahre sahn
als wär es Lug und Wahn.
die sind nun träg und alt.
verhauen ist der Wald.
so wie es weiland floß.
mein Unglück wäre groß.
der mich einst wohl gekannt.
wohl aus der Gnade Stand.
an manchen wonnigen Tag
wie in das Meer ein Schlag

*The Middle High German text is on p. 342

That he with me lay,
if they ever
knew it, (God forbid!) ashamed I'd be.
What he did, oh may
others never
find out the truth, but him and me,
and a friendly little bird,
tandaradei,
that will never say a word.

ALAS! WHERE HAVE THEY VANISHED, ALL THOSE YEARS OF MINE!

Alas! Where have they vanished all those years of mine!
Has my life been but a dreaming or a truth in fine?
What I believed e'er was something say, was all that aught?
It seems that I was sleeping and I knew it not.
Now I have awakened and to me is unknown
What before was familiar as this hand, my own.
People and land in which I was raised in days gone by
Have now become so foreign to me seem but a lie.
Those who were once my playmates have old and sluggish grown,
The forest is cut down the field lies scorched and blown.
Were not the water flowing as it did e'er flow,
In truth my wretchedness would now be great, I trow.
Now many men greet me slowly who once well recognized me.
The world is everywhere so full of misery.
Then I today remember many a joyful day,
Like a blow in the ocean from me now passed away,
Forevermore, alas!

ICH SASS AUF EINEM STEINE*

Ich saß auf einem Steine
Und deckte Bein mit Beine,
Darauf setzt ich den Ellenbogen,
Ich hatte in meine Hand geschmogen
Das Kinn und eine Wange,
So dachte ich mir recht lange,
Wie man wohl sollte leben.
Doch keinen Rat konnt ich mir geben,
Wie man drei Ding erwürbe,
Von denen keins verdürbe.
Die zwei sind Ehre und fahrend Gut,
Das eine dem andern Schaden tut,
Das dritte ist Gottes Huld,
Die Krone dieser beiden
Die wollt ich gerne in einen Schrein —
Doch dies kann leider niemals sein.
Dass Gut und weltlich Ehre
Und Gottes Huld noch mehre
Zusammen in ein Herz kann kommen.
Dahin sind Weg und Steg genommen
Verrat herrscht in der Gasse,
Gewalt fährt auf der Straße.
Friede und Recht sind nur zu wand.
Die drei verbleiben ohne Kraft, sind nicht die zwei vorher gesund.

*The Middle High German text is on p. 342

I SAT UPON A STONE

Upon a stone I sat
and crossed my legs so that
my elbow on my knee did rest,
then gently to my hand I pressed
my cheek, my chin in thought.
I long an answer sought
to how one on the earth should live,
and yet no counsel could I give,
how one three things obtains
that each unspoiled remains.
The honor and goods of life are two
that often each other damage do.
The third one is God's grace
on which more worth we place.
In one chest I would like all three,
but sadly it just cannot be
that wealth, world's honor sweet,
and God's grace e'er should meet
together in a single heart.
Their paths are all blocked from the start:
In ambush treachery hides,
on highways brute force rides,
justice and peace are wounded sore.
No escort the three will have until we first those two to health restore.

ABRAHAM A SANTA CLARA

DER MOND

Öfters muß des Mondes Schein,
Für die Menschen, schamrot sein,
(Monet rubicunda pudoris)

Es sind so Sonn als Mond des Himmels schönste Fackeln:
Die erste glänzt am Tag, die andre bei der Nacht.
Von jener muß das Feld voll Korn und Ähren wackeln,
Da dieser unsre Flut mit Fischen fruchtbar macht.
Die Sonne gleicht dem Gold, der Mond hat Silberschein;
Von beiden zieht die Welt den größten Nutzen ein.

Drum sollt man Nacht und Tag dem großen Schöpfer dienen –
Für Mondes Silberglanz, und für der Sonnen Gold.
Allein was tut man hier? Man schnarcht, wann sie erschienen;
Man bleibt dem kühnen Werk der Finsternüsse hold;
Man deckt die Laster zu mit schwarzem Flor der Nacht.
Das ist es, was den Mond so gar oft schamrot macht.

THE MOON

Frequently the moonlight's flame
Must for humans blush with shame.
(Monet rubicunda pudoris)

The sun and moon are both the heavens' fairest flares.
The first shines in the day, the second in the night.
Now from the first the field both ear and wheat-grain bears,
The second makes our streams with schools of fish alight.
The sun is like to gold, the moon has silver-sheen,
From both of them the world does greatest profit glean.

The great Creator's word men day and night should hear –
For Luna's silver-shine, and for the golden sun.
What do men do? They snore, when either will appear,
And to the work stay true that darknesses have done.
Their vices men conceal with ebon crepe of night:
It's this which often gives the moon its blushing light.

CATHARINA REGINA VON GREIFFENBERG

AUF DIE FRÖHLICH UND HERRLICHE AUFERSTEHUNG CHRISTI

Engel! blaset die Trompeten! Seraphinen / singt und klingt/
Jubil-Jubil-Jubilieret / hoch erfreuter Himmel-Chor!
Sonn und Sterne / glänzt und danzet eurem Triumphierer vor!
Berg' und Hügel / Fels und Türme/ auch in frohem Jauchzen springt!

Ihr für alls beglückte Menschen / weil es euch zu Heil gelingt /
Lobet / preiset / ehret / danket und erhebet hoch empor
Den / der sich und euch erhebet aus des Tods ins Himmels Chor.
Dann die paradeisisch Unschuld sein' Erstehung euch mitbringt.

Sollte wohl die Sündenmacht dessen Allmacht überstreben /
Der die selbst' Unendlichkeit? Nein, sie muss sich ganz ergeben:
Sein Verdienstes-Meer kann löschen / nicht nur Fünklein / ganze Feur.

Ach der lang verlangt' Erlöser tötet alle Ungeheur.
Was will Welt / Tod / Teufel / Höll einem Christen abgewinnen?
Die sind ganz verstört / verheert: Dieser herrscht im Himmel drinnen.

GOTT LOBENDE FRÜHLINGSLUST

Himmel voll Zimbel / voll Lauten und Geigen /
Bisem- und Amber'-erfüllete Luft /
Rosen- und Lilgen-verlieblichter Tuft!
Wollest / den Höchsten zu loben / nit schweigen!

Himmel an wolle die Süßheit aufsteigen /
Herrlich Gott ehrend aus tiefester Kluft.
Seine Genaden und Wunder ausruft /
Wie sie sich mächtig und prächtig erzeigen.

THE MOON

> Frequently the moonlight's flame
> Must for humans blush with shame.
> (Monet rubicunda pudoris)

The sun and moon are both the heavens' fairest flares.
The first shines in the day, the second in the night.
Now from the first the field both ear and wheat-grain bears,
The second makes our streams with schools of fish alight.
The sun is like to gold, the moon has silver-sheen,
From both of them the world does greatest profit glean.

The great Creator's word men day and night should hear –
For Luna's silver-shine, and for the golden sun.
What do men do? They snore, when either will appear,
And to the work stay true that darknesses have done.
Their vices men conceal with ebon crepe of night:
It's this which often gives the moon its blushing light.

CATHARINA REGINA VON GREIFFENBERG

AUF DIE FRÖHLICH UND HERRLICHE AUFERSTEHUNG CHRISTI

Engel! blaset die Trompeten! Seraphinen / singt und klingt/
Jubil-Jubil-Jubilieret / hoch erfreuter Himmel-Chor!
Sonn und Sterne / glänzt und danzet eurem Triumphierer vor!
Berg' und Hügel / Fels und Türme/ auch in frohem Jauchzen springt!

Ihr für alls beglückte Menschen / weil es euch zu Heil gelingt /
Lobet / preiset / ehret / danket und erhebet hoch empor
Den / der sich und euch erhebet aus des Tods ins Himmels Chor.
Dann die paradeisisch Unschuld sein' Erstehung euch mitbringt.

Sollte wohl die Sündenmacht dessen Allmacht überstreben /
Der die selbst' Unendlichkeit? Nein, sie muss sich ganz ergeben:
Sein Verdienstes-Meer kann löschen / nicht nur Fünklein / ganze Feur.

Ach der lang verlangt' Erlöser tötet alle Ungeheur.
Was will Welt / Tod / Teufel / Höll einem Christen abgewinnen?
Die sind ganz verstört / verheert: Dieser herrscht im Himmel drinnen.

GOTT LOBENDE FRÜHLINGSLUST

Himmel voll Zimbel / voll Lauten und Geigen /
Bisem- und Amber'-erfüllete Luft /
Rosen- und Lilgen-verlieblichter Tuft!
Wollest / den Höchsten zu loben / nit schweigen!

Himmel an wolle die Süßheit aufsteigen /
Herrlich Gott ehrend aus tiefester Kluft.
Seine Genaden und Wunder ausruft /
Wie sie sich mächtig und prächtig erzeigen.

CONCERNING THE JOYOUS AND SPLENDID RESURRECTION OF CHRIST

Angels, sound upon your trumpets! Seraph-armies, sing and ring!
Oh you rapturous band of Heaven, jubil-, jubil-, jubilate!
Sun and stars, before your Victor dancing, glancing celebrate!
Hill and mountains, cliff and towers, in your joyful triumph spring!

Race of man, by this salvation blest before each other thing,
Praise and worship, thank and honor, high aloft Him elevate,
Who within His person lifted you from death to Heaven's estate.
For to you His resurrection will a sinless Eden bring.

Should then his omnipotence 'gainst some sinful potence fall,
He Who is Eternity? No, for sin itself must fall:
Plunged into His sea of virtue sparks are quenched and mighty fire.

Oh, the long desired Redeemer makes the monster-band expire.
What gain of the Christian soul have the world, death, devil, hell?
It will reign in Heaven's manse; rack and ruin their empire fell.

SPRING-JOY PRAISING GOD

Sky full of cymbals, of fiddles and lutes,
Air that the musk and the ambergris fill,
Rose-scent and lily-breath lovelier still,
Cease not your praise of the Lord's attributes!

Sweetness, ascend on the heavenly routes,
Giving God honor from earth's deepest kill.
Cry out his grace, his miraculous will,
Showing how mighty, how bright are their fruits

Leset / in weisslichen Blättern der Blüh /
Göttlicher Allmacht ungleichliche Werke.
Sehet / in Traidern / die himmlische Stärke /

Die das Blüh-Härlein bewahret ohn Müh.
Göttliche Wunder in allem man siehet /
Wann man den Vorhang der Faulheit aufziehet.

DAS BEGLÜCKENDE UNGLÜCK

Es dunken uns zwar schwer die Creutz und Trübsal-Zeiten:
Jedoch sie / nach dem Geist / sehr nutzlich seynd und gut:
dieweil / den Palmen gleich / der Christlich Heldenmuht
sich schwinget hoch empor in Widerwärtigkeiten.
  Man pflegt mit großer Müh die Kräuter zubereiten /
eh man das Oel erlangt / der Kräuter Geist und Blut:
man brennt und läutert sie bey mancher heißer Glut.
So will uns Gottes Raht auch zu der Tugend leiten.
  Es muss das Spiegelglaß sehr wol geschliffen seyn /
sonst ist es nicht gerecht und wirffet falschen Schein.
der Mensch / in dem sich Gott bespiegelt / soll er leuchten /
  so muss durch Creutzes-Stahl er werden zugericht.
Allein in Unglücks-Nacht / siht man das Liecht im Liecht.
uns nutzt das Creutz / als wie dem Feld das Thaubefeuchten.

Read in the white-tinted leaves of the bloom
Godly omnipotence-works without peer.
See strength divine in the corn and the ear,

Easily guarding the bloom's tiny plume.
Heavenly wonders in all things one finds,
If he but raises his slothfulness' blinds.

FORTUNE-BRINGING MISFORTUNE

We think we cannot bear the times of cross and need,
Yet they are for the soul a goodly exercise.
For like unto the palm the Christian heart may rise,
And hover far above misfortune's hateful breed.
    It's custom of the cook his greens with care to knead,
Ere he their soul and blood, the oil, to them applies.
In many of flame they're thrust which burns and purifies.
Thus God's advice will us to virtue also lead.
    One must the mirror's glass well with the grinder ply,
Else it will not be right and casts its glance awry.
The man who is God's glass, if he will mirror true,
    Must through the cross's steel by pain be set aright;
In ruin's night alone one sees the light in light.
And to us is the cross as to the field the dew.

LAURENTIUS VON SCHNÜFFIS

LOBET IHR HIMMEL DEN HÖCHSTEN DORT OBEN

Lobet ihr Himmel den Höchsten dort oben,
Lobt in der Höhe ihn, bringet ihm Ehr:
All seine Engel die sollen ihn loben,
Lobet ihn alle sein heiliges Heer!
Lobet ihn Sonn und Mond, lobet ihn gerne.
Lobet ihn alle hell-leuchtende Sterne.

Lobet ihn alle ihr Himmel, ihr Seen,
Die ihr dort oben am Himmel her seyt!
Ihr solt den Nammen des HErren erhöhen
Dann es geschaffen wird, wann er gebeut:
Er macht, daß immer und ewig sie stehen,
Wie er sie ordnet, so müssen sie gehen.

Lobet den HErren, den Herrscher auff Erden,
Alle Ihr Wallfisch', und Tieffen so fort,
Hagel, Schnee, Feuer, Dampff, Sturmwind die werden
Richten aus seine Befehle und Wort,
Lobet ihn alles, was lebet und webet,
Lobet den Herrscher, der ewiglich lebet:

Alle ihr Berge und Hugel desgleichen,
Alle ihr Cedern und Bäume, die ihr
Grünet und blühet, gebt eu're Lobzeichen,
Vögel, Gewürme und allerley Thier,
Lobet ihr Fürsten und Könige alle
GOtt auff der Erden mit frölichem Schalle.

Alle ihr Richter, ihr Völcker und Zungen,
Die ihr auff Erde seyt nahe und ferrn,
Jüngling, Jungfrauen, auch Alte und Jungen
Lobet und preiset den Namen des HErrn,
Massen sein Name allein ist erhöhet,
Der, so weit Himmel und Erden ist, gehet.

PRAISE, OH YOU HEAVENS, THE HIGHEST ON HIGH

Praise, oh you heavens, the Highest on high /
   Praise Him and honor Him, praise all His ways:
Praise Him, you angels that people the sky /
   Armies of sainthood that sing in His praise!
Sun and moon, praise Him / and praise with delight,
Praise Him, you bright-shining stars with your light.

Praise Him, you heavens / celestial seas /
   Loftily stretching the length of the skies!
Lift up the name of the Lord without cease /
   At His word solely do all things arise:
That they're eternal is wrought by His deed /
As He arranges them, so they proceed.

Praise now the master who rules o'er the world /
   All you whale-fishes, you realms of the deep /
Hail and snow, fire and fog, stormwinds unfurled /
   Do but His bidding, His orders they keep.
All things must praise Him, of sea and of shore /
Praising the master Who lives evermore.

All you great mountains, you hills e'en the same /
   All you tall cedars, you other trees: mind
How you shall burgeon to signal His fame /
   Bird-folk and snake-folk and beasts of each kind /
Princes and potentates / sing with one voice:
Praise God on earth by your song, and rejoice.

All you stern judges, each people, each tongue /
   Which near and far in the world's circle dwell /
Youths and fair maidens, the old and the young /
   Raise the Lord's name and His praises retell.
For His name only is lifted on high /
Reaching the limits of earth and the sky.

Er hat das Horn seines Heils auffgerichtet
  Alle ihr Heiligen rühmet ihn drob,
Die ihr zum Dienste des Herrn euch verpflichtet,
  Preiset den Höchsten, erhebet sein Lob,
Ihr Zioniten, das Volck, das ihm dienet,
Singt: Hallelujah! ihr seyt nun versühnet.

He has exalted His salvation's horn /
  All saints assembled, proclaim Him therefore /
You to His service are pledged and reborn /
  Praise Him, the Highest, and praise Him still more.
Children of Zion, who serve at His feet /
Sing Hallelujah: your grace is complete.

MARTIN JOSEPH PRANDSTETTER

AN KLOEN

Du zürnest über nichts mit mir,
Und heißest gar mich gehen;
O glaub' es nur, du hast mich hier
Zum letztenmal gesehen.

Und schickst du, wie du drohtest, mir
Zurück die kleinen Lieder,
Gut, Stolze, gut, so geb' ich dir
Auch deine Küsse wieder.

DANKLIED

Meiner Vielgeliebten gleich
Giebt es nichts im weiten Reich.
 Eine beßre Beute
Macht kein Fürst, drum trag' ich sie
Auf den Händen, lasse nie
 Sie von meiner Seite.

Wenn noch kaum der Morgen graut,
Hängt die Liebliche vertraut
 Schon an meinem Munde.
O wie brennet sie für mich!
Wer ist froher dann als ich
 Auf dem Erdenrunde!

Dieses süsse Lippenspiel
Wird mir nimmermehr zu viel,
 Und in langen Zügen
Trink' ich sichtbar manche Stund'
Aus dem schöngeformten Mund
 Labung und Vergnügen.

TO CHLOE

You're angry over naught with me
   And even bid me leave;
Then here no more my face you'll see,
   And that you can believe.

If, as you threatened, by and by
   The songs you should return,
Then shall your kisses, proud one, I
   Give back to you in turn.

SONG OF THANKS

In the empire there is none
Like my much belovéd one.
   Not a better plunder
Makes a prince, and thus I bear
Her upon my hands, and ne'er
   Let her from me wander.

Scarce has morning's dawn begun,
Hangs by then my lovely one
   At my warm mouth here.
Oh, and how she burns for me!
Who'd more glad than I then be
   On this earth's broad sphere!

This sweet play of her lip's touch
Ne'er for me will be too much,
   Often even in plain sight
I, in deep and lengthy sips
Drink from her sweet well-formed lips
   Pleasure and delight.

Laß o Schicksal sie mir nur!
Sie ist mir von der Natur
   Eine süsse Gabe.
Feste, Gunst der grossen Herrn,
Tanz und Spiel verlaß' ich gern,
   Wenn ich sie nur habe.

Manches Silberkettchen wand
Meine pflegereiche Hand,
   Manches Band von Seiden
Um den schönen Hals; es muß,
Wer sie sieht, mir den Genuß,
   Meiner Holden neiden.

Schwirrt der Sorgen düstrer Schwarm
Mir vorm Auge, drückt der Harm
   Meine Seele nieder:
O dann fühl' ich ihren Werth!
Denn aus ihrem Munde kehrt
   Ruh' und Freude wieder,

Wenn sich laut und sorgenlos
In der biedern Freundschaft Schoos
   Meine Wünsch' ergiessen,
Red' ich vor ihr ohne Scheu;
Mein Geheimstes, was es sey,
   Darf sie alles wissen.

Abends bey des Mondes Schein
Lieg' ich oft mit ihr allein
   Hingestreckt im Grase;
Manches Mädchen, jung und schön,
Rümpft dann im Vorübergehn
   Über sie die Nase.

Immerhin! was kümmern mich,
Hab' ich, traute Freundinn, dich,
   Noch Eroberungen?
Drum hab' ich aus Dankbegier,
Meine Tobakspfeife, dir
   Dieses Lied gesungen.

Leave her, destiny, to me,
Nature's gift to me is she,
  Gift so sweet and fair.
Feasts, great lords' good will, believe,
Dance and game I gladly leave,
  If for me she's there.

Many a small silver chain
From my tending hand has lain,
  Oft a silken band,
Round her lovely neck; and he
Who sees her must envy me
  My fair pleasure grand.

When before me care's dark swarm
Buzzes there, when presses harm
  My soul down in pain;
O, then how I feel her worth!
Then return sweet peace and mirth
  From her lips again.

When my wishes noisily
In staunch friendship's bosom, free,
  Careless, overflow,
Deepest secrets utter I
There before her, never shy,
  She them all may know.

Evenings by the moon's cool shine,
Stretched on grasses soft and fine
  She with me reposes;
Many maidens young and fair
See her as they pass us there,
  Wrinkle up their noses.

Ne'ertheless, what need I more,
If you're mine, dear, why then for
  Other conquests long?
Thus have I in thanks to you,
My tobacco pipe so true,
  Sung this little song.

MARIANNE VON WILLEMER

AN DEN WESTWIND

Ach, um deine feuchten Schwingen,
West, wie sehr ich dich beneide:
Denn du kannst ihm Kunde bringen,
Was ich in der Trennung leide!

Die Bewegung deiner Flügel
Weckt im Busen stilles Sehnen;
Blumen, Augen, Wald und Hügel
Stehn bei deinem Hauch in Tränen.

Doch dein mildes, sanftes Wehen
Kühlt die wunden Augenlider;
Ach, für Leid müßt' ich vergehen,
Hofft ich nicht zu sehn ihn wieder.

Eile denn zu meinem Lieben,
Spreche sanft zu seinem Herzen;
Doch vermeid, ihn zu betrüben,
Und verbirg ihm meine Schmerzen.

Sag ihm, aber sags bescheiden,
Seine Liebe sei mein Leben;
Freudiges Gefühl von beiden
Wird mir seine Nähe geben.

TO THE WEST WIND

Ah, your dewy pinions swinging
Eastward, west wind I would borrow,
For I know that swiftly winging
You can tell him how I sorrow.

Here your swaying wings, oh Blower,
Wake a longing unresisted;
Eye and tree and hill and flower
At your breath in tears are misted.

Yet your wafting, mild and tender,
Cools the eyelids of their burning;
Ah, to grief I should surrender,
But for hope of his returning.

Then to my beloved hasten;
Whisper to his heart; but bidden
To forbear to grieve or chasten,
Wind, my pain from him keep hidden.

Tell, in manner unassuming,
My life is his love unshaken,
And of both a joyous blooming
Will his nearness for me waken.

ANONYM

PRINZ EUGEN

Prinz Eugenius, der edle Ritter,
Wollt dem Kaiser wiedrum kriegen
Stadt und Festung Belgerad.
Er ließ schlagen eine Brucken,
Daß man kunnt hinüberrucken
Mit der Armee wohl für die Stadt.

Als der Brucken nun war geschlagen,
Daß man kunnt mit Stuck und Wagen
Frei passiern den Donaufluß:
Bei Semlin schlug man das Lager,
Alle Türken zu verjagen
Ihn'n zum Spott und zum Verdruß.

Bei der Parole tät er befehlen,
Daß man sollt die Zwölfe zählen
Bei der Uhr um Mitternacht;
Da sollt all's zu Pferd aufsitzen,
Mit dem Feinde zu scharmützen,
Was zum Streit nur hätte Kraft.

Alles saß auch gleich zu Pferde,
Jeder griff nach seinem Schwerte,
Ganz still ruckt man aus der Schanz.
Die Musketier wie auch die Reiter
Täten alle tapfer streiten
Es war fürwahr ein schöner Tanz!

Ihr Konstabler auf der Schanzen,
Spielet auf zu diesem Tanzen
Mit Kartaunen groß und klein,
Mit den großen, mit den kleinen
Mit die Türken, auf die Heiden,
Daß sie laufen all davon!

PRINCE EUGENE

Prince Eugenius, the knight so noble,
Would get Belgrade's fortress, city
For the Emperor again.
Bridge o'er stream he had them throw
That across it one might go
Before the town with fighting men.

When the bridge was erected here
That one could with carts and gear
O'er the Danube stream pass free:
Near Semlin they camped that day,
Set to drive all Turks away,
Vex them with contumely.

At change of watch the order he sounded
That by them the twelve be counted
When the clock at midnight tolled;
Should mount up each of the men
With the foe to skirmish then,
All who had the strength to fight.

Mounted soon were all the men,
Each reached for his saber then,
Silent left they the redoubt.
The musketeers and riders too
All fought fearless, brave and true,
A lovely dance, without a doubt!

Gunners, you, on field-works staying
To this dance should now be playing
With your cannons large and small,
With the large ones, with the small ones,
At the Turkish, at the heathens,
That they all did run away!

ANONYM

O, DU LIEBER AUGUSTIN

O, du lieber Augustin,
s Geld is hin, s Mensch is hin,
O, du lieber Augustin,
Alles ist hin!

Wär schon des Lebens quitt,
Hätt ich nicht noch Kredit,
Aber so folgt Schritt für Schritt
Mir der Kredit!

Na, und selbst s reiche Wien,
Arm ist's wie Augustin,
Seufzt mit ihm im gleichen Sinn:
Alles ist hin!

Jeden Tag war sonst ein Fest,
Jetzt aber habn wir die Pest!
Nur ein großes Leichennest,
Das ist der Rest!

O, du lieber Augustin,
Leg nur ins Grab dich hin,
O, du mein herzliebes Wien,
Alles ist hin!

O YOU JOLLY AUGUSTINE

O you jolly Augustine
Money's gone, woman's gone
O you jolly Augustine,
Everything's gone.

I'd rid of life now be,
Were credit lost to me,
Yet quite unerringly
It follows me!

Even rich Vienna's here
Poor as dear Gus, I fear,
Sighs along with meaning clear:
All is gone here.

Each day was a feast day blessed,
But now we have the pest,
Just one big corpses' nest,
That is the rest!

O you jolly Augustine,
Lie down upon the bier,
My Vienna dear, so dear,
Nothing's left here!

FERDINAND RAIMUND

BRÜDERLEIN FEIN

Jugend Brüderlein fein, Brüderlein fein,
Mußt mir ja nicht böse sein!
Scheint die Sonne noch so schön,
Einmal muß sie untergehn,
Brüderlein fein, Brüderlein fein,
Mußt nicht böse sein.

Wurzel Brüderlein fein, Brüderlein fein,
Wirst doch nicht so kindisch sein!
Gib zehntausend Taler dir
Alle Jahr, bleibst du bei mir.

Jugend Nein, nein, nein, nein!
Brüderlein fein, Brüderlein fein,
Sag mir nur, was fällt dir ein?
Geld kann vieles in der Welt,
Jugend kauft man nicht ums Geld.
Drum, Brüderlein fein, Brüderlein fein,
's muß geschieden sein.

Beide.

Jugend Brüderlein, bald, Brüderlein, bald
Flieh ich fort von dir.

Wurzel Brüderlein, halt, Brüderlein, halt,
Geh nur nicht von mir.

Jugend Brüderlein fein, Brüderlein fein,
Wirst mir wohl recht gram jetzt sein?
Hast für mich wohl keinen Sinn,
Wenn ich nicht mehr bei dir bin?
Brüderlein fein, Brüderlein fein,
Mußt nicht gram mir sein!

MY BROTHER DEAR

Youth My brother dear, dear as can be,
     You must not be mad at me!
     Though the sun may lovely shine,
     It must yet at last decline.
     My brother dear, dear as can be,
     Be not mad at me.

Wurzel My brother dear, dear as can be,
     Not so childish be with me!
     I'll ten thousand thalers pay
     Every year, if you will stay.

Youth Nay, nay, nay, nay!
     My brother dear, will you but say,
     What you're thinking of, I pray?
     Though for money much is sold,
     Youth cannot be bought for gold.
     Thus, my brother dear, I can but say,
     We must part today.

     Both

Youth My brother, soon, my brother soon
     I shall from you flee.

Wurzel Dear brother, stop, grant me this boon,
     Please don't go from me.

Youth My brother dear, dear as can be,
     Will you now be cross with me?
     Will you think of me no more
     When I'm gone, far from your door?
     My brother dear, dear as can be,
     Don't be cross with me!

Wurzel Brüderlein fein, Brüderlein fein,
Du wirst doch ein Spitzbub sein!
Willst du nicht mit mir bestehn,
Nun, so kannst zum Teuxel gehn!

Jugend Nein, nein, nein, nein!
Brüderlein fein, Brüderlein fein,
Zärtlich muß geschieden sein.
Denk manchmal an mich zurück,
Schimpf nicht auf der Jugend Glück!
Drum, Brüderlein fein, Brüderlein fein,
Schlag zum Abschied ein!

Beide Brüderlein fein, Brüderlein fein,
Schlag zum Abschied ein!

LIED DES VALENTIN

Da streiten sich die Leut herum
Oft um den Wert des Glücks,
Der eine heißt den andern dumm,
Am End weiß keiner nix.
Da ist der allerärmste Mann
Dem andern viel zu reich.
Das Schicksal setzt den Hobel an
Und hobelt s' beide gleich.

Die Jugend will halt stets mit Gwalt
In allem glücklich sein,
Doch wird man nur ein bissel alt,
Da find't man sich schon drein.
Oft zankt mein Weib mit mir, o Graus!
Das bringt mich nicht in Wut.
Da klopf ich meinen Hobel aus
Und denk, du brummst mir gut.

Wurzel	My brother dear, my brother small,
	You'll a rogue be, after all!
	If you'll not stay with me, oh,
	To the devil you can go!
Youth	Nay, nay, nay, nay!
	My brother dear, let me now say,
	Fondly we must part today.
	Sometimes think of me and then
	Curse not at youth's joy again!
	Thus, my brother dear, shake hands, I pray,
	Ere we part this day.
Both	My brother dear, shake hands, I pray,
	Ere we part this day.

VALENTIN'S SONG

About the worth of happiness
The people oft have fought,
One scolds another's foolishness,
None in the end knows aught.
For one, the very poorest man
Has too much wealth and fame,
Fate sets its plane, as it but can,
and planes til they're the same.

Youth e'er seeks happiness untold
In everything by force.
Yet if one grows a little old,
One learns to cope, of course.
My wife scolds me quite often, Oh!
It brings no rage from me.
I tap my plane out, thinking so:
"Well, grumble on, feel free."

Zeigt sich der Tod einst mit Verlaub
Und zupft mich: Brüderl, kumm!
Da stell ich mich im Anfang taub
Und schau mich gar nicht um.
Doch sagt er: Lieber Valentin!
Mach keine Umständ! Geh!
Da leg ich meinen Hobel hin
Und sag der Welt Adje.

ABSCHIED

So leb denn wohl, du stilles Haus!
Ich zieh' betrübt von dir hinaus;
Ich zieh' betrübt und traurig fort,
noch unbestimt an welchen Ort.

So leb denn wohl, du schönes Land,
in dem ich hohe Freude fand!
Du zogst mich groß, du pflegtest mein
und nimmermehr vergeß ich dein!

So lebt denn all' ihr Lieben wohl,
von denen ich jetzt scheiden soll!
Und find' ich draußen auch mein Glück,
denk' ich doch stets an euch zurück.

If death comes sometime, by your leave,
Tugs: Brother, come with me!
At first then I will make believe
I'm deaf, won't turn to see.
But if, Dear Valentin, he says,
I want no fuss from you!
I'll put my plane down in its place
And bid the world adieu.

FAREWELL

So now, you quiet house, adieu!
Dejectedly I move from you;
dejected, sadly forth I go,
but whither still I do not know.

Farewell, you land of loveliness
in which I found great happiness!
You raised me and you nurtured me,
and ne'er you'll leave my memory!

Farewell then, all of you so dear,
from whom I now am parting here!
Though I out there my fortune find,
You'll never be far from my mind.

HERMANN VON GILM

ALLERSEELEN

Stell auf den Tisch die duftenden Reseden,
Die letzten roten Astern trag herbei
Und laß uns wieder von der Liebe reden,
    Wie einst im Mai.

Gib mir die Hand, daß ich sie heimlich drücke,
Und wenn man's sieht, mir ist es einerlei;
Gib mir nur einen deiner süßen Blicke,
    Wie einst im Mai.

Es blüht und funkelt heut' auf jedem Grabe,
Ein Tag im Jahre ist den Toten frei;
Komm an mein Herz, daß ich dich wieder habe,
    Wie einst im Mai.

DIE NACHT

Aus dem Walde tritt die Nacht,
An den Bäumen schleicht sie leise,
Schaut sich um im weiten Kreise –
    Nun gib acht!

Alle Lichter dieser Welt,
Alle Blumen, alle Farben
Löscht sie aus und stiehlt die Garben
    Weg vom Feld.

Alles nimmt sie, was nur hold;
Nimmt das Silber weg des Stromes,
Nimmt vom Kupferdach des Domes
    Weg das Gold.

ALL SOULS' DAY

The fragrant mignonettes place on the table,
The last red asters bring in soft array,
Let's speak again of love, if we are able,
      As once in May.

Give me your hand, let me in secret press it,
And if they see, I care not what they say;
But one sweet glance, to me, o please address it,
      As once in May.

On every grave today the blossoms shine,
We give the dead each year one holiday;
Come to my heart, that you'll again be mine,
      As once in May.

NIGHT

Night steps from the forest there,
Creeps on trees without a sound,
In wide circles looks around —
      Now beware!

All this world's lights once again,
Blossoms, colors it erases,
Steals the last beams from their places
      On the plain.

It takes all that's lovely, gay,
Takes the silver from the stream,
Takes the church roof's golden gleam
      Quite away.

Ausgeplündert steht der Strauch —
Rücke näher! Seel' an Seele,
O die Nacht, mir bangt, sie stehle
Dich mir auch.

EIN GRAB

Es liegen Veilchen dunkelblau
Auf einem Grab im Abendtau,
Ein kleines Mädchen kniet davor
Und hebt die Hände fromm empor:

„O sagt, ihr Veilchen, in der Nacht
Der Mutter, was der Vater macht,
Daß ich schon stricken kann und daß
Ich tausendmal sie grüßen laß."

Now the bush stands bare, stripped free,
Spirit nearer move to spirit!
O the night would steal, I fear it,
    You from me.

A GRAVE

The violets lie darkly blue
Upon a grave in even-dew.
A little maiden kneeling by
Lifts pious hands towards the sky:

"Tonight, you violets, o say
To Mother, what Dad's done today,
That I can knit already, bear
My thousand greetings to her there."

MARIE VON EBNER-ESCHENBACH

EIN KLEINES LIED

Ein kleines Lied! Wie geht's nur an,
Daß man so lieb es haben kann,
Was liegt darin? erzähle!

Es liegt darin ein wenig Klang,
Ein wenig Wohllaut und Gesang
Und eine ganze Seele.

GRABSCHRIFT

Im Schatten dieser Weide ruht
Ein armer Mensch, nicht schlimm noch gut.
Er hat gefühlt mehr als gedacht,
Hat mehr geweint als er gelacht;
Er hat geliebt und viel gelitten,
Hat schwer gekämpft und – nichts erstritten.
Nun liegt er endlich sanft gestreckt,
Wünscht nicht zu werden auferweckt.
Wollt Gott an ihm das Wunder tun,
Er bäte: Herr, o laß mich ruhn!

A LITTLE SONG

A little song! Why is it so,
That one for it such love can know,
What lies therein? O tell!

Within a song a little ring,
A little melody to sing,
And one whole spirit dwell.

EPITAPH

In shadows of this willow rests
A poor man, not the worst nor best.
He felt more than he ever thought,
More made him weep than laughter brought;
He suffered much, loved ere 'twas done,
He struggled hard and – nothing won.
Stretched softly in his final bed
Would not be wakened from the dead.
If God's grace would raise him anew,
He'd say: Lord, let me rest, please do!

NIKOLAUS LENAU

DER POSTILLION

Lieblich war die Maiennacht,
Silberwölklein flogen,
Ob der holden Frühlingspracht
Freudig hingezogen.

Schlummernd lagen Wies' und Hain,
Jeder Pfad verlassen;
Niemand als der Mondenschein
Wachte auf der Straßen.

Leise nur das Lüftchen sprach,
Und es zog gelinder
Durch das stille Schlafgemach
All der Frühlingskinder.

Heimlich nur das Bächlein schlich,
Denn der Blüten Träume
Dufteten gar wonniglich
Durch die stillen Räume.

Rauher war mein Postillion,
Ließ die Geißel knallen,
Über Berg und Tal davon
Frisch sein Horn erschallen.

Und von flinken Rossen vier
Scholl der Hufe Schlagen,
Die durchs blühende Revier
Trabten mit Behagen.

Wald und Flur im schnellen Zug
Kaum gegrüßt—gemieden;
Und vorbei, wie Traumesflug,
Schwand der Dörfer Frieden.

THE POSTILLION

Lovely was the night in May;
Silver clouds were flying
Over springtime's fair array
Far beneath them lying.

Sleeping lay both field and wood,
Lonely every byway;
No one but the moonlight stood
Watch upon the highway.

Only breezes spoke, and they
Tiptoe-still went creeping
Through the chamber where there lay
Springtime's children sleeping.

Secretly the brook slipped on,
Deep the perfumes breathing
That the flowers' dreams had thrown
Through the still night wreathing.

My postillion was less still;
Cracks his long whip's lashes;
Gaily over vale and hill
Bugle notes he flashes.

The four horses swiftly stride,
And with loud hoofs beating
Through the lovely countryside
Cheerily are fleeting.

Wood and field in rapid flight,
Hardly greeted, vanished.
And our speeding through the night
Dreamlike hamlets banished.

Mitten in dem Maienglück
Lag ein Kirchhof innen,
Der den raschen Wanderblick
Hielt zu ernstem Sinnen.

Hingelehnt an Bergesrand
War die bleiche Mauer,
Und das Kreuzbild Gottes stand
Hoch, in stummer Trauer.

Schwager ritt auf seiner Bahn
Stiller jetzt und trüber;
Und die Rosse hielt er an,
Sah zum Kreuz hinüber:

„Halten muß hier Roß und Rad!
Mag's euch nicht gefährden:
Drüben liegt mein Kamerad
In der kühlen Erden!

Ein gar herzlieber Gesell!
Herr, 's ist ewig schade!
Keiner blies das Horn so hell,
Wie mein Kamerade!

Hier ich immer halten muß,
Dem dort unterm Rasen
Zum getreuen Brudergruß
Sein Leiblied zu blasen!"

Und dem Kirchhof sandt' er zu
Frohe Wandersänge,
Daß es in die Grabesruh'
Seinem Bruder dränge.

Und des Hornes heller Ton
Klang vom Berge wieder,
Ob der tote Postillion
Stimmt' in seine Lieder.—

Suddenly a churchyard lay
Dark amid May's gladness,
Brought the wanderer on his way
Heavy thoughts and sadness.

Nestled to the mountainside
Lay the pale wall, by it
Stood the cross and Crucified
Sorrowful and quiet.

Now more sadly, now more still
Went my driver, turning
At the cross upon the hill
Glances full of yearning.

"Here must halt both horse and wheel—
Do not be astounded;
Yonder lies my comrade leal
Where the cool earth's mounded.

"He was aye a comrade dear;
What a shame he's left me.
None could blow a horn as clear—
Death has sore bereft me.

"I must always linger here,
To blow in loving greeting
To my sleeping comrade cheer,
Songs he loved repeating."

Wander-melodies he blew
Which had pleased the other
That they pierce the grave's peace through
To his sleeping brother.

When the bugle's echo rang
From the mountain clearly,
'Twas as if the sleeper sang
Songs he'd once loved dearly.

Weiter ging's durch Feld und Hag
Mit verhängtem Zügel;
Lang mir noch im Ohre lag
Jener Klang vom Hügel.

BITTE

Weil' auf mir, du dunkles Auge,
Übe deine ganze Macht,
Ernste, milde, träumerische,
Unergründlich süße Nacht!

Nimm mit deinem Zauberdunkel
Diese Welt von hinnen mir,
Daß du über meinem Leben
Einsam schwebest für and für.

DIE DREI

Drei Reiter nach verlorner Schlacht,
Wie reiten sie so sacht, so sacht!

Aus tiefen Wunden quillt das Blut,
Es spürt das Roß die warme Flut.

Vom Sattel tropft das Blut, vom Zaum,
Und spült hinunter Staub und Schaum.

Die Rosse schreiten sanft und weich,
Sonst flöss' das Blut zu rasch, zu reich.

Die Reiter reiten dicht gesellt,
Und einer sich am andern hält.

Sie sehn sich traurig ins Gesicht,
Und einer um den andern spricht:

Onwards then past field and fen,
Riverside and rillside,
Hearing ever and again
Yon echo from the hillside.

PRAYER

You dark eye, o rest upon me,
Exercise now all your might,
Earnest, mild and gentle, dreamy,
Sweet unfathomable night!

Do take with your magic darkness
This whole world away from me,
So that you above my life may
Lonely float eternally.

THE THREE

From a battle lost come riders three;
How gentle, how gentle the ride must be.

From mortal wounds pours down the blood,
The horses feel the warm red flood.

From saddle, from bridle the blood drops spray,
Washing the foam and dust away.

The steeds stride gently, soft and slow,
Else would the blood too richly flow.

Close pressed together, side by side,
They seek support as they slowly ride.

Sad they look in each other's eyes
And each to the other whispering sighs:

„Mir blüht daheim die schönste Maid,
Drum tut mein früher Tod mir leid."

„Hab' Haus and Hof und grünen Wald,
Und sterben muß ich hier so bald!"

„Den Blick hab' ich in Gottes Welt,
Sonst nichts, doch schwer mir's Sterben fällt."

Und lauernd auf den Todesritt
Ziehn durch die Luft drei Geier mit.

Sie teilen kreischend unter sich:
„Den speisest du, den du, den ich."

DIE DREI ZIGEUNER

Drei Zigeuner fand ich einmal
Liegen an einer Weide,
Als mein Fuhrwerk mit müder Qual
Schlich durch sandige Heide.

Hielt der eine für sich allein
In den Händen die Fiedel,
Spielte, umglüht vom Abendschein,
Sich ein feuriges Liedel.

Hielt der zweite die Pfeif' im Mund,
Blickte nach seinem Rauche,
Froh, als ob er vom Erdenrund
Nichts zum Glücke mehr brauche.

Und der dritte behaglich schlief,
Und sein Cimbal am Baum hing,
Über die Saiten der Windhauch lief,
Über sein Herz ein Traum ging.

"I have the fairest bride at home,
And so unwelcome death will come."

"House, hearth and forest green have I,
And yet here shortly must I die!"

"Just eyes to see God's world have I,
That's all; and yet it's hard to die."

Awaiting the end of the ride of death
Three vultures fly, and with greedy breath

They share their prey and screaming cry:
"Him you devour, him you, him I."

THE THREE GYPSIES

Once three gypsies I chanced to find
Camped by a willow together
As my carriage with lurch and grind
Toiled through the sand and the heather.

The one of them sat with his fiddle alone
And played with flying fingers
A little song with fire in its tone
In the light where the sunset lingers.

The second sat, pipe in his mouth,
And only its smoke he heeded,
As if on earth, north, west, east, south,
Nothing else for joy was needed.

In perfect comfort the third man slept;
On a three his zither apart swings;
Over its strings the wind's breath crept
And a dream over his heartstrings.

An de Kleidern trugen die drei
Löcher und bunte Flicken,
Aber sie boten trotzig frei
Spott den Erdengeschicken.

Dreifach haben sie mir gezeigt,
Wenn das Leben uns nachtet,
Wie man's verraucht, verschläft, vergeigt,
Und es dreimal verachtet.

Nach den Zigeunern lang noch schaun
Mußt' ich im Weiterfahren,
Nach den Gesichtern dunkelbraun,
Den schwarzlockigen Haaren.

On their clothes they wore, these three,
Rags in every condition;
But none the less defiantly free
They bade fate go to perdition.

In a threefold fashion the three of them say:
When life is melancholy,
Just smoke, or sleep, or fiddle it away
And thrice despise its folly.

To the gypsies long my eyes turned back
While my carriage onward paces,
Back to the locks of curly black,
Back to the swarthy faces.

ADALBERT STIFTER

HERBSTABEND

Der Herbstwind weht durch falbe Auen,
Das Abendrot ist blaß und kalt,
Zwei halberblichne Sterne schauen
Hernieder auf den Tannenwald
Zerstörte Wolkenbilder ziehn
Vereinzelt durch den Himmel hin,
Und kalte Abendnebel wehen
Von jenen ausgestorbnen Höhen.
Und was dein Auge keimen sah,
Zerstört ists, oder ist erkranket,
Nur daß in Stoppeln hie und da
Noch ein vergeßnes Hälmchen wanket.

Das Abendglöcklein tönt von ferne,
Wehmütig schwillt das Herz mir an.
Die Astern sehn mit traur'gem Sterne
Aus diesem Blumenbeet mich an.
Und wie des Ostes feuchter Hauch
Die Blätter regt am Fliederstrauch,
So flüstert es, wie eine Klage
Um längst vergangne Friedenstage.
Und fröstelnd bricht die Nacht herein,
Und Nebel dehnt sich dort am Teiche,
Und hüllt die toten Gründe ein,
Wie weiße Tücher eine Leiche.

AUTUMN EVENING

The fall wind blows through yellow leas,
The sunset glow is cold and pale,
Two half-spent stars above the trees
Look down on pinewood forest dale.
Demolished cloudbank pictures gray
Pass lonely through the sky away,
And frigid evening mists blow by
That come from those dead heights afly.
And what your eye saw budding fair,
Destroyed it is, diseased or rotten,
Except in stubble here and there
A little stem still sways forgotten.

The vesper bell rings from afar,
Now sadly swells my heart in me.
The asters look with dismal star
Up from this flower bed at me.
And as the east wind's moist, cool rush
The leaves moves on the lilac bush,
It whispers like a soft lament
For days of peace long past and spent.
And night now chilling closes in,
And fog spreads out there near the pool,
And cold, dead grounds are wrapped therein
As shroud a corpse cloths white and cool.

ANASTASIUS GRÜN

IM WINTER

Der Winter steigt, ein Riesenschwan, hernieder,
Die weite Welt bedeckt sein Schneegefieder.
Er singt kein Lied, so sterbensmatt er liegt,
Und brütend auf die tote Saat sich schmiegt;
Der junge Lenz doch schläft in seinem Schoß
Und saugt an seiner kalten Brust sich groß,
Und blüht in tausend Blumen wohl herauf,
Und jubelt einst in tausend Liedern auf.

So steigt, ein bleicher Schwan, der Tod hernieder,
Senkt auf die Saat der Gräber sein Gefieder,
Und breitet weithin über stilles Land,
Selbst still und stumm, das starre Eisgewand;
Manch frischen Hügel, manch verweht Gebein,
Wohl teure Saaten, hüllt sein Busen ein;
Wir aber stehn dabei und harren still,
Ob nicht der Frühling bald erblühen will?

IN WINTER

A giant swan descends: the winter weather,
The wide world's covered with its snowy feathers.
It sings no song, it lies so deathly weak
And brooding clings to sown fields dead and bleak;
Yet youthful spring is in its womb at rest
And growing suckles at its chilly breast,
And blooms up in a thousand flowers gay,
Rejoicing in a thousand songs one day.

Thus death, a pallid swan, is too descending,
Down on the seed of graves its feathers wending,
It spreads far o'er the country's silentness –
Itself still, dumb – the rigid icy dress;
Fresh grave mounds, many scattered bones there rest,
Dear seed indeed, enclosed within its breast,
But we all stand there waiting silently
And wonder if spring won't soon blooming be.

FERDINAND VON SAAR

SCHLUMMERLIED

Des Tages laute Stimmen schweigen,
Und dunkeln will es allgemach;
Ein letztes Schimmern in den Zweigen –
Dann zieht auch dies der Sonne nach.

Noch leuchten ihr Purpurgluten
Um jene Höhen, kahl und fern,
Doch in des Äthers klaren Fluten
Erzittert schon ein blasser Stern.

Ihr müden Seelen rings im Kreise,
So ist euch wieder Ruh gebracht;
Aufatmen hör' ich euch noch leis –
Dann küßt euch still und mild die Nacht.

HERBST

Der du die Wälder färbst,
Sonniger, milder Herbst,
Schöner als Rosenblühn
Dünkt mir dein sanftes Glühn.

Nimmermehr Sturm und Drang,
Nimmermehr Sehnsuchtsklang;
Leise nur atmest du
Tiefer Erfüllung Ruh.

Aber vernehmbar auch
Klaget ein scheuer Hauch,
Der durch die Blätter weht,
Daß es zu Ende geht.

LULLABY

Grown still loud voices of the day
   And darkness slowly dims the view;
In branches seems a gleam to stay—
   Then follows that the sunlight too.

Still glimmer there its purple glowings
   Around yon hilltop bare and far,
Yet in the ether's limpid flowings
   There trembles now a pallid star.

You weary souls around me here,
   To you is peace thus brought anew.
Your easy sighs, still soft, I hear,
   Then gently, still, night kisses you.

FALL

You who paints forests all,
Sunny and gentle fall,
Fairer than roses be,
Your soft glow seems to me.

Nevermore storm and stress,
Nor yearning's ringing press,
You breathe the quiet sound
Of peace fulfilled, profound.

But we hear with ease
Shy, a lamenting breeze
Mourn as through leaves it blows,
That it must reach its close.

WIEDER!

Wieder die ersten sonnigen Hauche,
    Lockend hinaus vor die düstere Stadt,
Wieder am zitternden, treibenden Strauche
    Die ersten Knospen, das erste Blatt.

Wieder auf leis' ergründenden Hängen
    Ersten Veilchens lieblicher Fund,
Wieder mit ersten Jubelgesängen
    Hebt sich die Lerche vom scholligen Grund.

Werdenden Frühlings verkündende Zeichen,
    Alte Genossen von Lust und Schmerz,
Ach, wie entzückt ihr, ihr ewig Gleichen,
    Ewig aufs neue das Menschenherz!

ALTER

Das aber ist des Alters Schöne,
    Daß es die Saiten reiner stimmt,
Daß es der Lust die grellen Töne,
    Dem Schmerz den herbsten Stachel nimmt.

Ermessen läßt sich und verstehen
    Die eigne mit der fremden Schuld,
Und wie auch rings die Dinge gehen,
    Du lernst dich fassen in Geduld.

Die Ruhe kommt erfüllten Strebens,
    Es schwindet des Verfehlten Pein —
Und also wird der Rest des Lebens
    Ein sanftes Rückerinnern sein.

AGAIN!

New, fresh again, the first sunny breeze
   Luring away from the city's dark gloom,
Push forth again on the shivering trees
   First leaf, first budding promise of bloom.

Once more where slowly greening slopes rise
   Is the first sweet violet found,
Raising in joy first songs to the skies
   Rises the lark once again from the ground.

Signs that the coming of spring now proclaim,
   Age old companions of joy and pain,
Ah, how you e'er, eternal the same,
   Gladden anew human hearts again.

AGE

Of age's beauty 'tis a measure
   That it more purely tunes the strings,
That it the harsher tones from pleasure
   Removes, from pain the sharpest stings.

It's possible to measure, know
   One's own guilt with another's sin,
However round you things may go,
   You learn true patience deep within.

Comes peace of struggles realized
   And failure's torment disappears –
Rememberings, now tender, prized,
   Become our life's declining years.

LANDSCHAFT IM SPÄTHERBST

Über kahle, fahle Hügel
Streicht der Dämmrung kühler Flügel;
Dunkel, wie erstarrte Träume,
Stehn im Tal entlaubt die Bäume.

Tiefe Stille, tiefes Lauschen;
Keine Welle hörst du rauschen,
Keine Stimme hörst du klingen,
Dir des Lebens Gruß zu bringen.

Nur als stummes Bild der Gnade
Siehst du dort am stein'gen Pfade,
Von des Kreuzes Holz getragen,
Durch die Nacht den Heiland ragen.

LANDSCAPE IN LATE AUTUMN

Over bare hills pale and still
Sweeps the wing of twilight chill;
Dark, in vales, like dreams congealed,
Trees stand leafless, limbs revealed.

Deep the slumber, deep the hush:
Not a wave do you hear rush,
Not a voice do you hear ring,
Life's salute to you to bring.

One lone symbol, mute, of grace
You see near that stony place,
Crucified, on wooden board,
Rising through the night, the Lord.

JOSEF MOHR

WEIHNACHTSLIED

Stille Nacht, heilige Nacht!
Alles schläft, einsam wacht
Nur das traute, hochheilige Paar;
Holder Knabe im lockigen Haar,
    Schlaf in himmlischer Ruh,
    Schlaf in himmlischer Ruh!

Stille Nacht, heilige Nacht!
Hirten erst kundgemacht
Durch der Engel Halleluja,
Tönt es laut von fern und nah:
    Christ, der Retter ist da,
    Christ, der Retter ist da!

Stille Nacht, heilige Nacht!
Gottes Sohn, o wie lacht
Lieb' aus deinem göttlichen Mund,
Da uns schlägt die rettende Stund,
    Christ, in deiner Geburt,
    Christ, in deiner Geburt!

CHRISTMAS SONG

Silent night, hallowéd night!
All's asleep, lonely sight,
Only watches the dear holy pair,
Fair young manchild with soft curly hair,
   Sleep in heavenly peace,
   Sleep in heavenly peace!

Silent night, hallowéd night!
Shepherds first knew the light
Through the angels' halleluja
Ringing loud from near and far,
   Christ, the Saviour is here,
   Christ, the Saviour is here!

Silent night, hallowéd night!
Son of God, o how bright
Smiles the love from Thy godly face
As for us strikes the hour of grace,
   Christ, our Lord, in Thy birth,
   Christ, our Lord, in Thy birth!

FRANZ GRILLPARZER

ZWISCHEN GAETA UND KAPUA

Schöner und schöner
Schmückt sich der Plan,
Schmeichelnde Winde
Wehen mich an;

Fort aus der Prosa
Lasten und Müh,
Flieg ich zum Lande
Der Poesie;

Goldner die Sonne,
Blauer die Luft,
Grüner die Grüne,
Würzger der Duft.

Dort an dem Maishalm,
Schwellend von Saft,
Sträubt sich der Aloe
Störrische Kraft.

Ölbaum, Cypresse,
Blond du, du braun,
Nickt ihr wie zierliche,
Grüßende Fraun?

Was glänzt im Laube,
Funkelnd wie Gold?
Ha, Pomeranze,
Birgst du dich hold!

Apfel der Schönheit,
Paris Natur
Gab dich Neapolis
Reizender Flur.

Ehrlicher Weinstock,
Nützest nicht bloß?
Schlingst hier zum Kranze den
Grünenden Schoß.

Überall Schönheit,
Überall Glanz,
Was bei uns schreitet
Schwebt hier im Tanz.

Trotzger Poseidon,
Wärest du dies,
Der drunten scherzt und
Murmelt so süß?

Und dies halb Wiese, halb
Äther zu schaun,
Es wär des Meeres
Furchtbares Graun?

Hier will ich wohnen!
Göttliche du,
Bringst du, Parthenope,
Wellen zur Ruh?

Nun, so versuch es,
Eden der Lust,
Ebne die Wogen
Auch dieser Brust!

BETWEEN GAETA AND CAPUA

Fairer and fairer
Is dressed out the lea,
Flattering breezes
Blow now at me;

Forth out of prose's
Burden and care,
I fly to land of
Poetry fair;

Goldener sunshine,
Bluer the skies,
Greener the verdure,
Scents with more spice.

There on the cornstalk,
Juices aflow,
Struggles the aloe's
Stubborn strength so.

Olive tree, cypress,
Blond and brunette,
Greet you like elegant
Ladies who've met?

What gleams in foliage,
Golden aglow?
Orange so lovely
Hiding, oho!

Apple of beauty,
Nature's Paris
Gave you to Naples'
Leas, the fairest.

Aren't you but useful,
Honest grapevine?
Here for a garland your
Green bosom twines.

Everywhere beauty,
Glow everywhere,
What at home strides, here
Dances on air.

Sulky Poseidon,
Are you the one
Who down there murmurs
So sweet in fun?

And this half meadow, half
Ether to see,
Could this the ocean's
Dread terror be?

Here I'll be dwelling!
Splendid one, best,
Can you, Parthenope
Bring waves to rest?

Well now, then try it,
Joy's Eden, you,
Smooth out the billows
In the breast too!

RICHARD VON SCHAUKAL

VORFRÜHLING

Fliegt ein Fink übern Pfad,
hüpft zum Bach durch den Busch,
nimmt ein flüchtiges Bad
und entschwindet im Husch.

Und ein Falter bewegt
immer gelber heran
sein Geflatter und legt
flach ans Gatter sich an.

Aber oben im Blau
spinnt die Sonne mit Macht,
hat die Rebstangen grau
schon zum Schimmern gebracht.

Dort am Hange im Hemd
mit der Harke der Mann
ist vom Licht überschwemmt
und blendet mich an.

Blitzt ein ragender Zweig
gar von weißestem Blühn.
Mir auf schlängelndem Steig
naht erwachendes Grün.

EARLY SPRING

Flies a finch o'er the path,
brookward hops through the bush,
takes a cursory bath,
disappears in a rush.

And a butterfly nears,
flutter yellower grows,
then it flattens, adheres
to the fence in repose.

But above in the blue
spins the sun with its might,
makes the vine stalk's gray hue
glow with shimmering light.

In his shirtsleeves up there
with his rake on that rise,
the man's bathed in a glare
that dazzles my eyes.

A high branch flashes gay
with the whitest blooms' sheen.
And on this winding way
nears me wakening green.

AN DEN HERRN

Du, in den wir münden,
du, aus dem wir erwacht:
wer, wer darf dich verkünden,
der du dich selbst erdacht!

Der du über den Zeiten
thronst in Unendlichkeit:
über die Meere gleiten
Schatten von deinem Kleid.

Tage und Nächte schleichen
unten an seinem Saum.
Erblühen und Verbleichen
gabst du uns als Traum.

TO THE LORD

You, to whom we flow,
you, from whom we arise:
who can proclaim, can know
you, who yourself devised.

You, who above the ages
throne in infinity:
gliding o'er oceans' rages
your robe's shadows we see.

Days and long nights are creeping
down here along its seams.
Our bloom, death's fading, sleeping,
you gave us as dreams.

RICHARD BEER-HOFMANN

SCHLAFLIED FÜR MIRJAM

Schlaf mein Kind – schlaf, es ist spät!
Sieh wie die Sonne zur Ruhe dort geht,
Hinter den Bergen stirbt sie im Rot.
Du – du weißt nichts von Sonne und Tod,
Wendest die Augen zum Licht und zum Schein –
Schlaf, es sind soviel Sonnen noch dein,
Schlaf mein Kind – mein Kind, schlaf ein!

Schlaf mein Kind – der Abendwind weht.
Weiß man, woher er kommt, wohin er geht?
Dunkel, verborgen die Wege hier sind,
Dir, und auch mir, und uns allen, mein Kind!
Blinde – so gehn wir und gehen allein,
Keiner kann keinem Gefährte hier sein –
Schlaf mein Kind – mein Kind, schlaf ein!

Schlaf mein Kind und horch nicht auf mich!
Sinn hats für mich nur, und Schall ists für dich.
Schall nur, wie Windeswehn, Wassergerinn,
Worte – vielleicht eines Lebens Gewinn!
Was ich gewonnen gräbt *mit* mir man ein,
Keiner kann keinem ein Erbe hier sein –
Schlaf mein Kind – mein Kind, schlaf ein!

Schläfst du, Mirjam? – Mirjam, mein Kind,
Ufer nur sind wir, und tief in uns rinnt
Blut von Gewesenen – zu Kommenden rollts,
Blut unsrer Väter, voll Unruh und Stolz.
In uns sind *Alle*. Wer fühlt sich allein?
Du bist ihr Leben – ihr Leben ist dein –
Mirjam, mein Leben, mein Kind – schlaf ein!

LULLABY FOR MIRJAM

Sleep, my child, it's late, go to rest.
Look how the sun sets in the west,
Over the mountains its last dying breath.
You—you know nothing of sun and of death,
Turning your eyes to light and to shine
Sleep, so many more suns are thine.
Sleep, my child, my child go to sleep.

Sleep, my child, the evening wind blows.
Nobody knows whence it comes, where it goes.
Dark and hidden the ways are here
For you, and for me and for all of us, dear!
Blindly we wander and wander alone,
No companion for you–or for me here below.
Sleep, my child, my child go to sleep.

Sleep, my child, and don't listen to me,
Meaning for me is but sounds for thee,
Sounds like the wind, like the falling of rain
Words–but may be a lifetime's gain.
All that I've reaped will be buried with me
None can to none an heir here be.
Sleep, my child, my child go to sleep.

Mirjam—my child, are you asleep?
We are but shores, and blood in us deep
Flows from those passed to those yet to be
Blood of our fathers restless and proud.
All are within us, who feels alone?
You are their life—their life is your own.
Mirjam, my life, my child go to sleep.

ALTERN

Graute dir nicht vor dem Baum, der
Immer nur in Blüte stände,
Ungerührt vom Gang der Zeiten,
Ewig starr in ihrer Wende?

Alle duftend weißen Blätter
Will die Blüte von sich streifen,
Tief im Kelch schläft ihr die Sehnsucht
Nach des Sommers heißem Reifen.

Von den sterngegrüßten Wipfeln
Zu den Wurzeln in der Erde
Kreist und pulst der tiefste Wille,
Daß die Blüte Frucht auch werde.

Blüte – Frucht – und wieder Samen!
Was ist Anfang, was ist Ende?
Nicht um ewiges Blühen hebe,
Flehend, du empor die Hände!

Wolle nicht, daß die da droben
Ewiger Satzung dich entbinden,
Fliehe nicht vor Vorbeschlossnem,
Stehe still – und laß dich finden!

Bebst zurück du vor dem Altern?
Schreckt dich eines Wortes Hall?
Sprich zum Stein nicht: ,,Du verwitterst!"
Wenn er reifet zum Krystal!

Fühle selig dich verschwistert
Du, dem Baum, dem Stern, dem Stein!
Furchtbar wär es, ausgeschlossen
Vom gemeinen Los zu sein!

AGING

Would you not be awed by trees
In eternal bloom sublime
Undisturbed by passing seasons
Changeless in the flow of time?

Shedding all its fragrant petals
Is a blossom's deep desire,
In its core an ardent longing
Sleeps for summer's ripening fire.

From the treetops touched by starlight
To the darkness' earthy roots
Circles, pulsates deepest yearning
That the blossoms turn to fruits.

Blossom, fruit, and see again –
What's beginning? What is ending?
Do not lift your hands in prayer
For the bloom's eternal splendor.

Do not crave that those above you
From eternal laws exempt you;
Do not flee from what's ordained;
Stay serene and let fate find you.

"Aging" – does it make you tremble?
Does this word fill you with fear?
Do not tell the stone "you crumble"
When it grows to crystal clear.

Feel the blessing of your kinship
With a tree, a star, a stone –
Dreadful curse to be excluded
From the common fate, alone.

Sterne, die ins Weite kreisen,
Kennen Unten nicht noch Oben –
Raum, wie Zeit: Gespinnst, Gespenster,
Die die Sinne um dich woben!

Blühen, Welken, Tod und Leben,
Kerker, die du dir gemauert!
Brich sie, tritt hinaus ins Freie,
Wo dich klare Luft umschauert!

Dir zu Häupten, dir zu Füßen –
Stern, der steht – und Stern, der irrt!
Alle kreisen! Tritt zu ihnen!
Keiner war – und jeder wird!

Stars that circle in their orbit
Do not know an "up" and "down."
Space and time are webs and phantoms
Which your senses weave around.

Blooming, wilting, dying, living:
Prison walls put up by you!
Break them – step into the open,
Where the air is clear and true.

Far above and deep below you
Stars seem still, stars seem revolving;
All are circling – join their cycle
None has been, all are evolving.

ARTHUR SCHNITZLER

SPRÜCHE IN VERSEN

Zur Ermutigung

So unvermeidbar ein Geschick dir scheine,
Neig ihm dein Haupt in frommer Demut nie,
Was heute sich des Schicksals Maske lieh,
War gestern *vieler* Möglichkeiten eine,
Und wird heut ohne dich die Wahl gefällt,
Von *morgen* die ist dir anheimgestellt.

Treib weit hinaus . . .

Treib weit hinaus auf raschem Kahn
An schwülem Sommertage;
Die Mücken, die dir weh getan,
Sind nur des Ufers Plage.

Beethovenfeier

Laßt Nachsicht walten, wenn ich auf Geheiß
Den Göttlichen nicht mitzufeiern weiß.
In Tempel tret' ich lieber schweigend ein
Und—wenn ihr mir's vergönnen wollt—allein.

Wortspirale

Die Wortspirale drehst du nie zu Ende;
Und ob um eine Spule sie aus Gold
Ob um ein Härchen, ob um nichts sie rollt, —
Eh du's erkundet, sinken dir die Hände.

Frühling im Herbst

Daß immer süßer dir von Jahr zu Jahre
Ins durst'ge Herz der Trank des Frühlings glitt, —
Begreifst du's nun, das Schmerzlich-Wunderbare?
Den bittern Tropfen Abschied trinkst du mit!

SAYINGS IN VERSE

Encouragement

However sure a fate may seem to be,
Your head in pious meekness never bend,
What fortune's mask to it today did lend,
Before was *just one* possibility,
And if without you choice is made today,
It's left to you to choose *tomorrow's* way.

Push Far Out . . .

Push far out in a swift canoe
On a sultry summer day;
Mosquitoes that gave pain to you
A plague on shore will stay.

Beethoven Celebration

Have patience if I know not on command
How I should fête one so divinely grand.
The shrine I'd rather enter silently
And when—if you'll permit—there's none but me.

Word Spiral

Word spiral's end—you'll find it nevermore;
And whether it around a spool of gold,
Or round a tiny hair, round nothing's rolled,—
Your hands will sink ere you can it explore.

Spring in Autumn

That ever sweeter slipped the draught of spring
Each year into the thirsty heart of you,—
Do you grasp now that painful wondrous thing?
The bitter drops of parting you drink too!

Nachwelt

Mag doch mein Name in nichts verklingen! —
Wenn sie nur meine Lieder singen!

Unsterblichkeit

Gehn die Jahrhunderte hin, verlischt auf dem Grabstein dein Name —
Wär' er in Goldschrift geprägt; und auch der Marmor zerfällt.
Doch es entblühn deinem Staub noch in den entlegensten Lenzen
Ewigen Duftes gewiß, Blumen von Faltern umschwebt.

Posterity

My name away to naught may ring!—
If only they my songs will sing!

Immortality

Onward the centuries press, your name on the tombstone grows faded—
If it were stamped there in gold; and too the marble decays.
But there will bloom from your dust still in the most far future springtimes
Sure of eternal perfume, flowers round which butterflies float.

ERNST GOLL

KÖNIGSZUG

Ihr, die ihr blinden Aug's vorübergeht,
Oh, daß ihr doch die Lider höbt und säht

In Morgenfrühe, wenn das Dunkel fällt,
Den Königszug der Jugend in die Welt.

Die Augen heiß, die Stirnen weinumlaubt
Und Fahnenwimpel über unserm Haupt,

So ziehn wir aus, den Sonnenweg entlang,
Und unser Lied ist Frühlingssturmgesang:

Du, Vater, in dem engbegrenzten Haus,
Sieh, unsre Sehnsucht breitet Schwingen aus!

Du, Mutter, die uns eng umfangen hält,
Hör, unser Herz gehört der ganzen Welt.

Ihr, die ihr hoffnungsleer an Gräbern steht
Und taumelt zwischen Arbeit und Gebet,

Das Zepter rollt aus eurer schwachen Hand:
Wir sind die Könige im weiten Land.

Zu lichten Höhen ziehen wir hinan,
Verneigt euch tief und gebt uns frei die Bahn!

Ihr aber mit dem warmen Augenglanz,
Ihr aber mit dem Margeritenkranz,

Ihr, die ihr schmachtend steht am Straßensaum,
Ihr seid das Licht in unserm Königstraum.

Oh, wartet nicht, bis unser Herz verglüht,
Oh, wartet nicht, bis euer Kranz verblüht!

ROYAL PROCESSION

You, who now pass blind-eyed, uncaringly,
Oh, that you'd raise your lids just once and see

In early morning, when the dark is furled,
The royal march of youth into the world.

Our eyes so hot, our foreheads garlanded,
And flags and pennants waving overhead,

We thus march out, the sunny way along,
And our own hymn is springtime's tempest song:

You, Father, in the narrow house and drear,
See, our deep yearning spreads its pinions here!

You, Mother, whose arms tightly us enfold,
Hear, this whole world within our hearts we hold.

You, standing there at graves, who hopeless feel,
And so between your prayer and labor reel,

The scepter rolls forth from your feeble hand:
We are the kings here now in this broad land.

To shining heights we're moving upward now,
Make way for us and deep before us bow!

But you with glowing eyes so warm and fair,
You with the wreath of daisies standing there,

You, who at highway's edge stand languishing,
You, in our royal dream light everything.

Wait not until our heart's bright glow is gone,
Wait not until your garland's bloom is wan!

Wir sind voll Sehnsucht. Reicht uns glückbereit
Den tiefen Becher eurer Seligkeit!

Ihr, die ihr blinden Aug's vorübergeht,
Oh, daß ihr doch die Lider höbt und säht . . .

HERBSTLICHE FÜLLE

Der Tag ist müde worden vom Verschwenden,
Er schlief mit roten Kinderwangen ein –
Not ruht auf meinen sonnverbrannten Händen
Und meine Seele gärt wie junger Wein.

Ich will die Kleider von den Gliedern streifen,
Nackt über die beschwerten Hänge gehn
Und nach der dunkelsten der Trauben greifen,
Die aus dem Gold- und roten Laube sehn.

Dann bin ich eins mit dieser Hügelweite,
Die tiefste Blüte aus dem Erntekranz
Und bete, daß dein Fuß darüberschreite
In dieser Nacht voll Duft und Mondenglanz.

We're filled with longing. Glad, in readiness,
Give us the chalice of your happiness!

You, who now pass blind-eyed, uncaringly,
Oh, that you'd raise your lids just once and see . . .

AUTUMN FULLNESS

From squandering, the day at length grew weary,
With childlike cheeks flushed red, to sleep it went—
Upon my sunburned hands rests trouble dreary,
And like new wine does my soul now ferment.

I'd strip the clothing now from off my members,
And naked o'er the laden slopes I'd go
And reach for darkest grapes that from the embers
Of red and golden foliage peer and glow.

Then I, the harvest garland's deepest flower,
Am one with this broad hilly countryside,
And pray that in this scentfilled moonlit hour
Of night your foot may also o'er it stride.

BLÜTEN

Geht ein Windhauch durch den weißen Flieder,
Hundert Blütensterne regnen nieder.
Einer schwebt und fällt auf meine Hand . . .
Bist du eines nahen Glückes Pfand?
Oder bringst du eine leise Mahnung,
Daß des viel zu frühen Todes Ahnung
Diese Stunde mich wie dich gestreift? –

BLOSSOMS

Passes wind through where white lilacs flower,
Blossom-stars a hundred downward shower.
Floats one there and falls upon my hand . . .
Do you for impending fortune stand?
Or bring you a quiet admonition
That of death too early premonition
Touched in this same hour both you and me? –

RICHARD BILLINGER

WIR BAUERN

Wir Bauern dulden keinen Spott
an unserm Herrn und Helfer Gott!

Was wären wir wohl ohne ihn?
Eine Ehschaft ohne Gatten.
Ein Bienstock ohne Königin.
Ein Baum ohne Frucht und Schatten.

Wir brauchen ihn wie's lötig Gold.
Der Bettler und der Eigenhold
kann nur „Vergelts Gott" sagen.
Dem Blinden scheinet hell sein Licht.
Er ists, der mit dem Kranken spricht.
Er hört des Stummen Klagen.

Er warf die Lerche in die Luft.
Er gab der Blume Farb und Duft.
Er gab dem Korn die halmende Kraft,
dem Apfel allen süßen Saft,
dem Bauern Macht und Leidenschaft
zum Werk, dem menschenguten.
Er hat die Ewigkeit verliehn.
Wir alle müßten ohne ihn
am Acker Zeit verbluten.

WE PEASANTS

We peasants tolerate no word
that mocks our helper, God our Lord.

What would we then without Him be?
A marriage with no husband there.
A beehive that has no queen bee.
A shadeless tree, fruitless and bare.

We need Him like the purest gold.
The bondsman and the beggar old
can naught but "God bless" say.
His light shines brightly for the blind.
In his words sick men comfort find.
He hears the voiceless pray.

He threw the lark up in the air,
gave flowers color and fragrance fair.
He gave the grain the power to grow,
from apples let sweet juices flow,
gave peasants strength and passion's glow
for work that man's good yields.
He gave the world eternity.
Without Him all would bleeding be
to death upon time's fields.

DIE SOLDATENBRAUT

Zur Abendzeit, vorm Schlafengehn,
Die Augen mir voll Tränen stehn.

Hab all die Stunden dein gedacht.
Wo hältst du Wache in der Nacht?

Ich brach das Brot, ich trank den Wein,
Wer bringt dir Speis, wer schenkt dir ein?

Wer sorgt um dich, wer hat des acht
Ob du geschluchzt, ob du gelacht?

Wein ich mir auch die Augen rot,
Was gilt dies wider deine Not?

Mein Bettlein ist von weichem Daun
Und deines ist die Erde braun.

Läg ich auf brauner Erd bei dir,
Ein Rosenteppich schien sie mir.

Läg ich mit dir auf Grabesgrund,
So wär doch nahe Mund zu Mund.

Zur Abendzeit, vorm Schlafengehn,
Die Augen mir voll Tränen stehn!

THE SOLDIER'S BETROTHED

At night-time, ere I go to sleep,
My eyes fill up with tears, I weep.

Through all the hours I've thought of you.
Where keep you watch the long night through?

I broke the bread, I drank the wine,
Who'll see that you will drink and dine?

Who cares for you, or if you would
Indulge in sobs or laughing mood?

Although my eyes are red with tears
What matters this beside your fears?

My bed is of the softest down
And yours is of the earth so brown.

On brown earth lying with you here,
A rosy bed it would appear.

If in the grave I lay with thee,
Then mouth to mouth so close we'd be.

At night-time, ere I go to sleep,
My eyes are filled with tears, I weep.

MAX FLEISCHER

REICHE ERNTE

Die Garben sind schon reif zum Binden.
Die Teiche liegen kühl und klar.
In dunstverhüllten Ackergründen
Entzündet sich ein reiches Jahr.

Wetz' deine Sensen, feg' die Tenne;
Der Sommer flieht schon wälderwärts.
Schür' deine Herzglut, daß sie brenne,
Der Winter naht, mein Sommerherz.

RICH HARVEST

The sheaves are ripe now for the tying.
The ponds and pools lie cool and clear.
In fields o'er which a haze is lying
Is kindled now a rich, full year.

Your scythes whet, sweep the threshing floor;
The summer forestward departs.
Your heart's fire stoke, let burn the more;
The winter nears, my summer-heart.

ANTON WILDGANS

ICH BIN EIN KIND DER STADT

Ich bin ein Kind der Stadt. Die Leute meinen,
Und spotten leichthin über unsereinen,
Daß solch ein Stadtkind keine Heimat hat.
In meine Spiele rauschten freilich keine
Wälder. Da schütterten die Pflastersteine.
Und bist mir doch ein Lied, du liebe Stadt!

Und immer noch, so oft ich dich für lange
Verlassen habe, ward mir seltsam bange,
Als könnt' es ein besondrer Abschied sein;
Und jedesmal, heimkehrend von der Reise,
Im Zug mich nähernd, überläuft's mich leise,
Seh' ich im Dämmer deine Lichterreihn.

Und oft im Frühling, wenn ich einsam gehe,
Lockt es mich heimlich-raunend in die Nähe
Der Vorstadt, wo noch meine Schule steht.
Da kann es sein, daß eine Straßenkrümmung,
Die noch wie damals ist, geweihte Stimmung
In mir erblühen macht wie ein Gebet.

Da ist der Laden, wo ich Heft und Feder,
Den ersten Zirkel und das erste Leder
Und all die neuen Bücher eingekauft,
Die Kirche da, wo ich zum ersten Male
Zur Beichte ging, zum heiligen Abendmahle,
Und dort der Park, in dem ich viel gerauft.

Dann lenk' ich aus den trauten Dunkelheiten
Der alten Vorstadt wieder in die breiten
Gassen, wo all die lauten Lichter glühn,
Und bin in dem Gedröhne und Geschrille
Nur eine kleine ausgesparte Stille,
In welcher alle deine Gärten blühn.

I AM A CITY CHILD

I am a city child – and folks agree
(and lightly ridicule the ones like me),
that such a town child has no homeland here.
Into my games there surely sighed no tones
of forests. Clattered there the cobblestones,
yet you're to me a song, you city dear.

And even now, as oft as I've departed
from you for long, I've felt strange, fearful-hearted,
as though a special parting it could be.
And every time, from travels then returning,
my train draws near, I'm moved by that soft yearning,
when I your rows of lights in twilight see.

And oft when I walk lonely in the spring
the suburb secretly is beckoning
to where my school still stands. Then it can be
that there some turn or winding in the street
that still is as it was, may cause a sweet
and hallowed mood to bloom prayerlike in me.

There is the shop where I my notebook, pen,
first compass and first leather purchased then,
along with all the new books that I bought,
the church where I first to Confession went,
where I first took the Holy Sacrament,
and there the park in which I often fought.

Then from the dear obscurities inside
the old outskirts I turn into the wide
roadways, where all the lights so brightly glow,
and am amid the roar, amid the shrillness
alone, a small reserve and untouched stillness
in which your gardens all now bloom and grow.

Und bin der flutend-namenlosen Menge,
Die deine Straßen anfüllt mit Gedränge,
Ein Pünktchen nur, um welches du nicht weißt;
Und hab' in deinem heimatlichen Kreise,
Gleich einem fremden Gaste auf der Reise,
Kein Stückchen Erde, das mein Eigen heißt.

AKKORD

In meiner Kindheit leisem Wiegentraum,
vor einem Fenster, licht und flügelbreit,
steht grün und golden ein Kastanienbaum.

Voll Lichtertanz und Huschen war der Raum,
und oben schien der Himmel klar und weit
und krönte jedes Ding mit Silbersaum –
nimm deine Geige, Frau Vergangenheit . . .

Da sprachen sie zu mir mit holdem Laut,
und lieber Blick hat hell auf mir geruht,
und selbst das Fremde kam und ward vertraut.

Und wenn ich Schiff und Festung mir gebaut,
erhitzt vom ersten Schöpferübermut,
hat mir die Mutter heimlich zugeschaut,
und sicher fand sie, was ich baute, gut.

Seit damals sah ich nimmer diesen Raum,
dort wohnt jetzt andrer Menschen Glück und Leid,
und auch das Haus, die Straße weiß ich kaum.

Nur aus der Kindheit leisem Wiegentraum,
vor einem Fenster, licht und flügelbreit,
grüßt grün und golden ein Kastanienbaum –
nimm deine Geige, Frau Vergangenheit . . .

And am the nameless crowd that floods along,
that fills your streets, that presses here in throng,
I'm just a speck that is to you unknown,
and in your native circle here have I,
just like a foreign guest come travelling by,
no bit of earth that I can call my own.

CHORD

In gentle childhood cradle dream I see
before a window, light and spreading so,
there standing green and gold a chestnut tree.

Light filled the room there, flitting, dancing free,
and broad above the sky did limpid glow,
crowned everything with border silvery –
Dame Past, take up your violin and bow . . .

They spoke to me with gracious sound and phrase,
and precious glance upon me rested bright,
the strange came, grew familiar in its ways.

And when I ship and fortress then did raise
with first creative arrogance alight,
my mother looked at me with stealthy gaze
and surely found what I built good and right.

The room I after that no more did see,
there dwell now other people's joy and woe,
the house and street are hardly known to me.

But in my gentle childhood dream I see
before a window, light and spreading so,
there greeting green and gold a chestnut tree –
Dame Past, take up your violin and bow . . .

LETZTE ERKENNTNIS

Willst du gleich die Früchte greifen?
Hast doch eben erst gesät!
Laß sie werden, laß sie reifen:
Früh ist Arbeit, Ernte spät.

Läßt kein Wachstum sich beschleunen,
Ihr Gesetz hat jede Saat,
Rüste Werkzeug, baue Scheunen
Für die Fechsung, für die Mahd!

Heimsen andre Pflüger eher,
Voll Geheimnis ist die Welt;
Sei kein Neider, sei kein Späher
Nach des Nachbars Ackerfeld!

Glaubst du vor dem Schnitt zu sterben,
Sei nicht bange um die Frucht!
Kein Ertrag bleibt ohne Erben,
Keine Tat bleibt ungebucht.

Wer im Werk den Lohn gefunden,
Ist vor Leid und Neid gefeit,
Denn er hat sich überwunden
Und kann warten und hat Zeit.

FINAL KNOWLEDGE

Would you grasp the fruits already?
You've just sown, now you must wait!
Let them ripen til they're ready,
Work is early, harvest late.

Its own law has every sowing,
No growth's rushed along its way,
For the vintage, for the mowing
Build the barns, and tools array!

Be there others sooner reaping,
This world's full of mystery;
You not envying, not peeping
At your neighbor's field should be!

Ere all's reaped, if you be dying,
For the fruit then do not fear!
No crop's left without heirs vying,
No deed stays uncounted here.

Who work as reward has counted
Is immune to envy, pains,
For he has himself surmounted
And can wait, his time remains.

MAX MELL

HEIMAT

Die Heimat lädt dich ein.
Sei zu ihr lieb!
Es könnte einmal sein,
es könnte einmal sein,
daß nichts dir blieb;

Daß Lockung log und Glast,
die Ferne starrt so leer;
was du gewonnen hast,
was du gewonnen hast,
kennst du nicht mehr.

Die Heimat ließ dich nicht!
Und sei es, daß du erst
zu ihr im Abendlicht,
zu ihr im Abendlicht
aufatmend kehrst.

Sie zeigt mit keuscher Kraft
dir ihre traute Welt,
und drüber riesenhaft,
und drüber riesenhaft
ihr Sternenzelt.

HOMELAND

The homeland beckons you.
To her be kind!
One day it could be true,
One day it could be true,
You'd nothing find;

That lurings lied and gleam,
void stares the foreign shore;
what you once won, 'twill seem
what you once won, 'twill seem
you know no more.

Home did not from you go!
Be it that you first turn
to her by evenglow,
to her by evenglow
relieved return.

With strength of virtue she
shows to you her dear world,
with high vast canopy,
with high vast canopy
of stars unfurled.

FELIX BRAUN

WIE LANGE—?

Wie lange werden deine Augen bei dir sein?
Siehe – dein Haar weissagt dir schon die blassen Zonen
Der Wintersterne, wo du bald mußt wohnen,
Ohne der schönen Sonne Liebesschein.
Wie lange werden deine Augen bei dir sein?

Wie lange für dich lächeln wird dein Mund?
Sieh – deine Füße prüfen schon die tiefen Treppen,
Die ganz hinunter dich der Knechte Arme schleppen,
Dich hinzustrecken auf den schwarzen Grund.
Wie lange für dich lächeln wird dein müder Mund?

Wie lange weilt in deiner Brust dein Ich?
Die fremden Schwestern aus den unfaßbaren Welten
Hausen in unsern Herzen wie in Wanderzelten
Und brechen jählings auf und flüchten sich.
Wie lange, meine Seele, bleibst du noch mein Ich?

HOW LONG?

How long will your eyes be with you? Oh, do you know?
See – your hair already the pallid zones foretells
Of winter stars, up where you soon must dwell
Without the lovely sun's own loving glow.
How long will your eyes be with you? Oh, do you know?

And just how long will smile for you your mouth?
See – your own feet already test the downward stair,
Where you, way down, men in their arms will bear,
Upon the dark black earth to lay you out.
And just how long will smile for you your weary mouth?

How long within your breast will your self stay?
The eerie sisters from worlds that none comprehends
Dwell within our own hearts as in wander-tents
And suddenly set out and flee away.
How long then, my own soul, will you still my self stay?

ALFRED MARGUL-SPERBER

DER TAG DER LANDSCHAFT

Der Morgen stand im Brand der Wolkenröten.
Sein Haupt hob schimmernd sich aus Duft und Tau.
Er trug im Haar den Sang der Hirtenflöten
und Vogelstimmen durch den Glanz der Au.

Der Mittag war ein flammendes Verstummen.
Durch die gelähmte Stille schläfrig klang
das Dengeln einer Sense und das Summen
der Bienenschwärme auf dem Wiesenhang.

Der Abend kam wie eine goldne Träne.
Die letzten Winde wiegten sich zur Ruh,
und durch die Bläue glitten Wolkenschwäne
verklärt und selig ihrer Heimat zu.

Dann sank die Nacht herab auf sanfter Schwinge,
das Antlitz überströmt von Sternenlicht.
Sie streichelte das Heimweh aller Dinge,
und jedes ward Geheimnis und Verzicht.

THE DAY OF THE LANDSCAPE

Ablaze in reddened clouds there stood the morning.
Aglow it raised its head from scent and dew.
With song of shepherds' flutes its hair adorning,
through meadow-gleam it bore birds' calls anew.

The midday was a flaming silence burning.
Through palsied stillness rang so sleepily
the whetting of a scythe, the humming, yearning
of swarms of bees upon the sloping lea.

A golden tear, the evening then descended.
The last soft breezes rocked themselves to rest,
and through the azure skies the cloud-swans wended
their gliding way toward home, transfigured, blest.

On gentle wind the night came downward pressing.
Across its face was starlight streaming free.
It was all things' nostalgia carressing,
and each became resigned, a mystery.

PAULA LUDWIG

JAHRESNEIGE

Die Linde ist schon lang verblüht
doch steht ihr Innres noch voll Duft

Das Julifeuer ist verglüht
doch wärmt es noch die dunkle Luft

Gesang der Grille ist verstummt
doch zittert noch im Gras ihr Lied

Noch eine goldne Biene summt
um Blumen – die es nicht mehr gibt –

Am Waldessaum erschrickt ein Wild
vor einem Baume – der entlaubt

Im Weiher spiegelt sich sehr mild
der Sonnenblume schwarzes Haupt –

Vom Rauch der Hütten angelockt
die zahme Herde talwärts wankt

Vom Strauch die bittre Beere brockt
die alte Hand – die nicht mehr dankt –

Der Wandrer prüft des Himmels Blau
und zögert mit dem leichten Schritt –

Am Ufer winkt noch eine Frau
dem Segel nach – das längst entglitt –

Des Landmanns Auge zieht den Kreis
noch einmal um die ganze Flur

und sinnt ein Wort – das niemand weiß
als jener – der vorüberfuhr

END OF THE YEAR

Although the lime's long faded, wan
its heart is full of fragrance fair

July's fire now is dead and gone
yet it still warms the dusky air

The cricket's song has died away
yet trembles in the grass its song

Still hums a golden bee today
round flowers – that no more exist –

At wood's edge starts a red deer wild
before a tree that's standing bare

In pond is mirrored gently, mild
black head of helianthus there

By smoke of cottages drawn nigh
the tame herd seeks the valley floor

From bush is bitter fruit picked by
the ancient hand – that thanks no more

The hiker checks the heaven's blue
and hesitates with easy stride

On shore a woman waves yet too
at sail – that long since forth did glide

The farmer's eye in circle goes
once more around the meadow there

and thinks a word – that no man knows
but he – who once did past him fare

Des sommerlichen Fischers Boot
ist nun von großen Dingen leer

was er noch fing im Abendrot
wirft er zurück ins weite Meer –

The summer angler's boat below
is now of larger objects free

What he still caught in sunset glow
he throws back in the great wide sea —

HERTA FELICIA STAUB

SEPTEMBER

September, der du rot und gold
kommst königlich gegangen,
mit Nächten, die der Sturm durchtollt,
mit Fernen, die weit aufgerollt
den Horizont umfangen;

der du des Sommers Müdigkeit
am schlaffen Grün erkennst
und alles, was zum Tod bereit,
im Taumel und voll Festlichkeit
hochlodernd rings verbrennst:

Du schreitest von Erfüllung schwer,
du nimmst und gibst zugleich.
Du breitest Gnade um dich her
und mahnst zu reifer Wiederkehr
ins dunkle Schattenreich.

SEPTEMBER

September, you who red and gold
come striding like a king,
with nights through which storms frolic bold,
with distances that broadly rolled
the far horizon ring;

you who the summer's weariness
in limp green come to know
and all that's ripe for death's caress
in rapture, full of festiveness
burn up in flaming glow:

You heavy with fulfillment pace,
you take and give as well.
Around you here you spread your grace,
remind to seek anew the place
where darkling shadows dwell.

CHRISTINE BUSTA

MEIN GELIEBTER...

Mein Geliebter ist der Sommer. Riesig schifft er
auf den Strömen hin und wirft nach beiden Seiten
Sonnengarben in die Felderbreiten
und den Rebenhügeln an die Brust.
Wenn er hingeht, Wiesen um die Lenden,
trägt er Bienenschwärme hoch in seinen Händen
und die Winde schimmern durch sein Haar.

Schön ist mein Geliebter, froh und hilfreich: trifft er
Wandrer oder Bettler, labt er sie mit Birnen,
hängt den Schläfern Laub über die Stirnen,
schenkt den Mägden Kränze bunter Lust.
Die Erschlafften badet er mit Regen,
füllt verdorrte Brunnen neu mit kühlem Segen
und mit Sternen das erprobte Jahr.

Einsam hausen wir zuletzt auf klaren Bergen,
tief in Wäldern. Weiße Wolkenfergen
bringen Botschaft aus gestillter Welt.
Und mit sanften Moosen, reifen Beeren
lehrt er mich das Innigste gewähren,
bis der Herbst aus meinem Schoße fällt...

MY BELOVED ...

My belovèd is the summer. Vastly sails he
down the rivers, and he throws on either side
sheaves of sunlight into fields so wide,
to the bosom of the vineyard hills.
When he goes, loins clad in meadowlands,
he bears swarms of bees on high there in his hands
and the breezes shimmer through his hair.

Handsome is my lover, glad and helpful: meets he
beggars, wanderers, he them with pears relieves,
over sleepers' foreheads he hangs leaves,
gives the maidens wreaths of colored joy.
What is languishing he bathes with rain,
fills the dried-up springs with blessing cool again,
and with stars above the proven year.

Lonely dwell we then at last upon clear heights,
deep in forests. Ferry-clouds of white
bring us word from sated world that calls.
He with berries ripe, with mosses tender,
teaches me what's innermost to render,
'til the autumn from my bosom falls ...

DEM LIEBEN GOTT

Gib mir auf Erden, Herr, nur so viel Raum,
wie Liebende ihn brauchen, still zu ruhn,
und zeige Blumen mir und Tier und Baum,
in lautrer Demut Dein Gesetz zu tun.

Du weißt, der große Sang ist nicht mein Teil,
mein Lied steigt nicht auf rauschendem Gefieder,
es fliegt nur wie ein leichter, goldner Pfeil
nach Deinem Licht und sinkt im Grase nieder:

Am Bach vielleicht, wo – wenn der Abend blinkt –
arglose Rehe ihn mit Staunen schaun,
oder ein Vogel ihn zum Busche bringt
wie einen Halm, damit sein Nest zu baun.

TO THE DEAR LORD

Give me on earth, Lord, only as much room
as lovers need in order to rest still,
and show me animal and tree and bloom,
in pure humility to do Thy will.

You know, the great grand song is not my part,
my song does not on rushing feathers rise,
it flies but like a light and golden dart
toward Thy light, in grass then sinking lies:

Near brook perhaps, where – when the evening blinks –
it's seen by guileless deer with wonder filled,
or else a bird it to the bushes brings
just like a straw, with it its nest to build.

INGEBORG BACHMANN

DIE GROSSE FRACHT

Die große Fracht des Sommers ist verladen,
das Sonnenschiff im Hafen liegt bereit,
wenn hinter dir die Möwe stürzt und schreit.
Die große Fracht des Sommers ist verladen.

Das Sonnenschiff im Hafen liegt bereit,
und auf die Lippen der Galionsfiguren
tritt unverhüllt das Lächeln der Lemuren.
Das Sonnenschiff im Hafen liegt bereit.

Wenn hinter dir die Möwe stürzt und schreit,
kommt aus dem Westen der Befehl zu sinken;
doch offnen Augs wirst du im Licht ertrinken,
wenn hinter dir die Möwe stürzt und schret.

THE GREAT FREIGHT

The great freight of the summer now is loaded,
the sun-ship ready in the harbor lies,
when back of you the seagull dives and cries.
The great freight of the summer now is loaded.

The sun-ship ready in the harbor lies,
and on the lips of bowsprit figures here
the smiles of lemurs undisguised appear.
The sun-ship ready in the harbor lies.

When back of you the seagull dives and cries,
comes from the west the order to sink down;
yet open-eyed you will in brightness drown,
when back of you the seagull dives and cries.

GEORG TRAKL

VERKLÄRTER HERBST

Gewaltig endet so das Jahr
Mit goldnem Wein und Frucht der Gärten.
Rund schweigen Wälder wunderbar
Und sind des Einsamen Gefährten.

Da sagt der Landmann: Es ist gut.
Ihr Abendglocken lang und leise
Gebt noch zum Ende frohen Mut.
Ein Vogelzug grüßt auf der Reise.

Es ist der Liebe milde Zeit.
Im Kahn den blauen Fluß hinunter
Wie schön sich Bild an Bildchen reiht –
Das geht in Ruh und Schweigen unter.

EIN WINTERABEND

Wenn der Schnee ans Fenster fällt,
Lang die Abendglocke läutet,
Vielen ist der Tisch bereitet
Und das Haus ist wohlbestellt.

Mancher auf der Wanderschaft
Kommt ans Tor auf dunklen Pfaden.
Golden blüht der Baum der Gnaden
Aus der Erde kühlem Saft.

Wanderer tritt still herein;
Schmerz versteinerte die Schwelle.
Da erglänzt in reiner Helle
Auf dem Tische Brot und Wein.

EFFULGENT AUTUMN

With golden wine and gardens' fruit
The year so potently is ending.
The wondrous woods around are mute
Companions to the lonely rending.

Then says the peasant: It is good.
You vespers long and softly ringing
At day's end lend a joyous mood.
A flock of birds then greets while winging.

The time of gentle love is there.
While down the azure river rowing,
How picture joins with picture fair –
Down into peace and silence going.

A WINTER EVENING

When the snow falls near the panes,
Long ring vespers o'er the gable,
Set for many is the table,
In the house good order reigns.

Many travelers come here,
Reach the gate through darkness pressing,
Golden blooms the tree of blessing
From the earth's juice cool and clear.

Wand'rer enters with soft tread;
And the sill turned pain to stone.
Glow with brightness all their own
On the table wine and bread.

DER HERBST DER EINSAMEN

Der dunkle Herbst kehrt ein voll Frucht und Fülle,
Vergilbter Glanz von schönen Sommertagen.
Ein reines Blau tritt aus verfallner Hülle;
Der Flug der Vögel tönt von alten Sagen.
Gekeltert ist der Wein, die milde Stille
Erfüllt von leiser Antwort dunkler Fragen.

Und hier und dort ein Kreuz auf ödem Hügel;
Im roten Wald verliert sich eine Herde.
Die Wolke wandert überm Weiherspiegel;
Es ruht des Landmanns ruhige Gebärde.
Sehr leise rührt des Abends blauer Flügel
Ein Dach von dürrem Stroh, die schwarze Erde.

Bald nisten Sterne in des Müden Brauen;
In kühle Stuben kehrt ein still Bescheiden
Und Engel treten leise aus den blauen
Augen der Liebenden, die sanfter leiden.
Es rauscht das Rohr; anfällt ein knöchern Grauen,
Wenn schwarz der Tau tropft von den kahlen Weiden.

AUTUMN OF THE LONELY

The dark fall comes with fruit and fullness piled,
Of lovely summer days the yellowed glow.
From pods decayed steps blue that's undefiled;
Birds' flight lets ancient tales ring out below.
The wine is pressed, now is the stillness mild
Filled with dark questions' answers soft and low.

And here and there a cross on hilltop bare;
In forest red a herd is disappearing.
Above the pond a cloud roves through the air;
Now rests the peasant's calm and quiet bearing.
Blue wing of evening touches softly there
A dried straw roof and black earth in the clearing.

'Neath weary brows soon nest stars from the skies;
In cool rooms still contentment comes to be
And angels softly step out of blue eyes
Of lovers who endure more tenderly.
Then rustle reeds; and bony fears arise,
When black the dew drips from bare mead and lea.

HUGO VON HOFMANNSTHAL

VORFRÜHLING

Es läuft der Frühlingswind
Durch kahle Alleen,
Seltsame Dinge sind
In seinem Wehn.

Er hat sich gewiegt,
Wo Weinen war,
Und hat sich geschmiegt
In zerrüttetes Haar.

Er schüttelte nieder
Akazienblüten
Und kühlte die Glieder,
Die atmend glühten.

Lippen im Lachen
Hat er berührt,
Die weichen und wachen
Fluren durchspürt.

Er glitt durch die Flöte
Als schluchzender Schrei,
An dämmernder Röte
Flog er vorbei.

Er flog mit Schweigen
Durch flüsternde Zimmer
Und löschte im Neigen
Der Ampel Schimmer.

Es läuft der Frühlingswind
Durch kahle Alleen,
Seltsame Dinge sind
In seinem Wehn.

EARLY SPRING

There runs the wind of spring
Through avenues bare,
Strange and peculiar things
Are blowing there.

It softly has swayed
Where people wept,
And cuddled and played
In hair loose and unkept.

From locusts it's shaken
The blossoms sweet
From breathing limbs taken
The glowing heat.

Lips that were merry
It has caressed,
Through fields soft and airy
Followed its quest.

Through flutes it came gliding,
A sobbing soft cry,
On evenglow riding
It flew on by.

In silence flying
Through whisp'ring low,
It blotted while dying
The lamplight's glow.

There runs the wind of spring
Through avenues bare,
Strange and peculiar things
Are blowing there.

Durch die glatten
Kahlen Alleen
Treibt sein Wehn
Blasse Schatten.

Und den Duft,
Den er gebracht,
Von wo er gekommen
Seit gestern Nacht.

DIE BEIDEN

Sie trug den Becher in der Hand
– Ihr Kinn und Mund glich seinem Rand –,
So leicht und sicher war ihr Gang,
Kein Tropfen aus dem Becher sprang.

So leicht und fest war seine Hand:
Er ritt auf einem jungen Pferde,
Und mit nachlässiger Gebärde
Erzwang er, daß es zitternd stand.

Jedoch, wenn er aus ihrer Hand
Den leichten Becher nehmen sollte,
So war es beiden allzu schwer:
Denn beide bebten sie so sehr,
Daß keine Hand die andre fand
Und dunkler Wein am Boden rollte.

ÜBER VERGÄNGLICHKEIT

Noch spür ich ihren Atem auf den Wangen:
Wie kann das sein, daß diese nahen Tage
Fort sind, für immer fort, und ganz vergangen?

Dies ist ein Ding, das keiner voll aussinnt,
Und viel zu grauenvoll, als daß man klage:
Daß alles gleitet und vorüberrinnt.

Through unbladed
Avenues going
Drives its blowing
Shadows faded.

And the scent
Brought in its flight
From whence it's been coming
Since yesternight.

THE TWO

The cup she carried in her hand
– Her mouth was like its border – and
So light and certain was her stride,
There sprang no droplet from inside.

So light and solid was his hand:
He rode upon a fine young horse,
And with a careless gesture's force
He made it stop and trembling stand.

However, when he then essayed
To take the light cup from her hand,
For both of them it weighed too much:
The two of them were trembling such
That hand with hand no contact made
And dark wine poured out on the land.

ON TRANSITORINESS

Her breath, I feel it still upon my face:
How can it be that these near days are borne
Away, forever lost without a trace?

Something none can fully comprehend,
And much too terrible for us to mourn,
That everything glides by, flows to an end.

Und daß mein eignes Ich, durch nichts gehemmt,
Herüberglitt aus einem kleinen Kind
Mir wie ein Hund unheimlich stumm und fremd.

Dann: daß ich auch vor hundert Jahren war
Und meine Ahnen, die im Totenhemd,
Mit mir verwandt sind wie mein eignes Haar,

So eins mit mir als wie mein eignes Haar.

PROLOG ZU DEM BUCH „ANATOL"

Hohe Gitter, Taxushecken,
Wappen nimmermehr vergoldet,
Sphinxe, durch das Dickicht schimmernd ...
... Knarrend öffnen sich die Tore. –
Mit verschlafenen Kaskaden
Und verschlafenen Tritonen,
Rokoko, verstaubt und lieblich,
Seht ... das Wien des Canaletto,
Wien von siebzehnhundertsechzig ...
... Grüne, braune, stille Teiche,
Glatt und marmorweiß umrandet,
In dem Spiegelbild der Nixen
Spielen Gold- und Silberfische ...
Auf dem glattgeschornen Rasen
Liegen zierlich gleiche Schatten
Schlanker Oleanderestämme;
Zweige wölben sich zur Kuppel,
Zweige neigen sich zur Nische
Für die steifen Liebespaare,
Heroinen und Heroen ...
Drei Delphine gießen murmelnd
Fluten in ein Muschelbecken ...
Duftige Kastanienblüten
Gleiten, schwirren leuchtend nieder
Und ertrinken in den Becken ...
... Hinter einer Taxusmauer
Tönen Geigen, Klarinetten,

And that my very self, by nothing bound
Could flow across and from a child descend,
To me, like some strange dog that makes no sound.

That I a hundred years ago was there,
That my ancestors, lying in the ground,
Are as akin to me as my own hair.

As much a part of me as my own hair.

PROLOGUE TO THE BOOK "ANATOL"

Lofty railings, taxus hedges,
Coats of arms, no longer gilded,
Sphinxes through the thicket gleaming . . .
. . . Creaking now the gates swing open –
Drowsy waterfalls cascading,
Sleepy groups of sculptured tritons,
Rococo, dust-covered, lovely,
See . . . the Vienna of Canaletto,
Vienna of the seventeen-sixties . . .
. . . Green and brown the ponds so quiet,
Smooth and marble-white surrounded,
In the sea nymphs' mirror image
Play the gold and silver fishes . . .
On the lawn cut smooth and even
Lie the dainty level shadows
Of the slender oleanders:
Branches rise to cambered ceiling,
Branches to the niche are bending
For the rigid loving couples,
Heroines there with their heroes . . .
Murmuring three dolphins pour out
Water in a mussel basin . . .
Sweetly fragrant chestnut blossoms
Gliding humming glowing downward
And they drown there in the basin . . .
. . . From behind a wall of taxus
Ring the clarinets and fiddles,

Und sie scheinen den graziösen
Amoretten zu entströmen,
Die rings auf der Rampe sitzen,
Fiedelnd oder Blumen windend,
Selbst von Blumen bunt umgeben,
Die aus Marmorvasen strömen:
Goldlack und Jasmin und Flieder . . .
. . . Auf der Rampe, zwischen ihnen
Sitzen auch kokette Frauen,
Violette Monsignori . . .
Und im Gras, zu ihren Füßen
Und auf Polstern, auf den Stufen
Kavaliere und Abbati . . .
Andre heben andre Frauen
Aus den parfümierten Sänften . . .
. . . Durch die Zweige brechen Lichter,
Flimmern auf den blonden Köpfchen,
Scheinen auf den bunten Polstern,
Gleiten über Kies und Rasen
Gleiten über das Gerüste,
Das wir flüchtig aufgeschlagen.
Wein und Winde klettert aufwärts
Und umhüllt die lichten Balken,
Und dazwischen farbenüppig
Flattert Teppich und Tapete,
Schäferszenen, keck gewoben,
Zierlich von Watteau entworfen . . .
Eine Laube statt der Bühne,
Sommersonne statt der Lampen,
Also spielen wir Theater,
Spielen unsre eignen Stücke,
Frühgereift und zart und traurig,
Die Komödie unsrer Seele,
Unsres Fühlens Heut und Gestern,
Böser Dinge hübsche Formel,
Glatte Worte, bunte Bilder,
Halbes, heimliches Empfinden,
Agonieen, Episoden . . .
Manche hören zu, nicht alle . . .
Manche träumen, manche lachen,

And they seem now from the charming
Amoretti to be streaming
That sit round us on the apron,
Fiddling there or plaiting flowers,
They themselves by flowers surrounded,
Streaming from the marble vases
Gold wallflower, jasmine, lilacs . . .
. . . On the apron there between them
Also sit flirtatious women,
Monsignori robed in purple . . .
At their feet, in grass below them,
And on cushions, on the stairway
Gallant cavaliers and abbots . . .
Others lift still other women
From sedan chairs fragrant, scented . . .
. . . Through the branches lights are breaking,
On blond heads they softly glimmer,
Shining on the colored cushions,
Gliding over grass and gravel,
Gliding there across the scaffold,
That we hastily erected.
Vine and bindweed clamber upward
and enwrap the open rafters,
And between them rich in color
Flutter tapestry and carpet
Shepherd scenes all boldly woven
By Watteau designed so neatly . . .
Stage is here replaced by arbor,
Summer sun instead of stage lights,
This is how we play our roles out,
Acting dramas of our making,
Early-ripe and sad and tender,
The commedia of our spirit,
What we feel as time slips by us,
Ugly facts in pretty guises,
Words so smooth and colored pictures,
Half-felt feelings sensed in secret,
Agonies and episodes . . .
Many listen here, not all do . . .
Many dream, and some are laughing,

Manche essen Eis ... und manche
Sprechen sehr galante Dinge ...
... Nelken wiegen sich im Winde,
Hochgestielte, weiße Nelken,
Wie ein Schwarm von weißen Faltern,
Und ein Bologneserhündchen
Bellt verwundert einen Pfau an.

Many eat ice cream . . . and many
Very gallant things are saying . . .
. . . In the breeze carnations sway there,
Long-stemmed lovely white carnations,
Like a swarm of white moths floating,
And a small Bolognese puppy
Barks in wonder at a peacock.

RAINER MARIA RILKE

HERBSTTAG

Herr: es ist Zeit. Der Sommer war sehr groß.
Leg deinen Schatten auf die Sonnenuhren,
Und auf den Fluren laß die Winde los.

Befiehl den letzten Früchten voll zu sein;
Gib ihnen noch zwei südlichere Tage,
Dränge sie zur Vollendung hin und jage
Die letzte Süße in den schweren Wein.

Wer jetzt kein Haus hat, baut sich keines mehr.
Wer jetzt allein ist, wird es lange bleiben,
Wird wachen, lesen, lange Briefe schreiben
Und wird in den Alleen hin und her
Unruhig wandern, wenn die Blätter treiben.

DER PANTHER

Im Jardin des Plantes, Paris

Sein Blick ist vom Vorübergehn der Stäbe
So müd geworden, daß er nichts mehr hält.
Ihm ist, als ob es tausend Stäbe gäbe
Und hinter tausend Stäben keine Welt.

Der weiche Gang geschmeidig starker Schritte,
Der sich im allerkleinsten Kreise dreht,
Ist wie ein Tanz von Kraft um eine Mitte,
In der betäubt ein großer Wille steht.

Nur manchmal schiebt der Vorhang der Pupille
Sich lautlos auf –. Dann geht ein Bild hinein,
Geht durch der Glieder angespannte Stille –
Und hört im Herzen auf zu sein.

AUTUMN DAY

Lord: it is time. The summer was so grand.
Lay Thy cool shadow out upon the sundials,
And let the winds be loosed upon the land.

Command the last fruits to be full and fine;
And give them yet two southerly warm days,
Press them on to perfection then and raise
The final sweetness in the heavy wine.

Who has no house, will build none now, I know.
Who now is lonely, so will long remain,
Will watch and read, long letters write in vain,
And through the streets will wander to and fro,
Uneasy, when the wind drives leaves again.

THE PANTHER

In the Jardin des Plantes, Paris

The passing of the bars has made his glance
So weary, that it nothing more contains,
As though there were a thousand bars perchance,
While past the thousand bars no world remains.

The strong and supple strides in gentle pace
That in the very smallest circle turns,
Are like a dance of force around a place
In which enormous will bewildered burns.

At times the pupil's curtain opens there
Unheard –. An image enters quietly
And passes through the limbs' strained silence, where
It ceases in the heart to be.

KARL KRAUS

UNTER DEM WASSERFALL

Wer vor mir ließ von diesem Wasserfall,
von dieser Sonne sich begnaden!
Wer vor mir stand, das Haupt im All,
stolz an der Ewigkeit Gestaden!

Von Gott bin ich hier eingeladen,
so hoch in Gunst wie jedes Tier,
und hier ist niemand außer mir,
hier will ich frei von mir mich baden!

Was ich mir selbst schuf, nahm mich selbst nicht auf,
und Wort und Weib, sie wiesen nach den Schatten
und alles Leben wurde ein Ermatten,
zurück in mich lief meiner Welten Lauf.

Nun bin ich zu den Wundern heimgegangen
und auf der Gotteswelt allein.
Hier dieser Sonnenstrahl ist mein.
Wie hat die Schöpfung festlich mich empfangen!

Lust ohne Leiden, Liebe ohne Last,
Naturdrang ohne Scham und Schranken –
ich bin an Gottes goldnem Tisch zu Gast
und hab' mir nichts mehr zu verdanken!

Weit hinter mir ist alles Weh und Wanken.
Wie hat der Wasserfall Bestand!
Wie segnet dieses Sonnenland
vor meiner Nacht mir die Gedanken!

UNDER THE WATERFALL

Who here before me by this waterfall
by this sun let himself blessed be!
Who stood before me, head held tall
proud at the shores of eternity!

Here God Himself invited me,
as favored now as any beast,
there's no one here but me at least,
here I me from myself shall free!

What I for me wrought did not me include,
and woman, word did to the shadows press,
and all of life became a weariness,
back to me ran all life that I'd pursued.

I now back to the wonders have retreated,
and in God's world I'm all alone.
This ray of sunlight is my own.
How splendidly creation me has greeted!

Joy without suff'ring, love that's burden-free,
life's craving without shame and fetter –
at God's gold table I'm a guest, you see,
am to myself no more a debtor!

All faltering and pain lie far behind.
O how the waterfall persists!
How this land blesses, sunlight-kissed,
before my night thoughts in my mind!

VOR EINEM SPRINGBRUNNEN

Villa Torlonia

Wie doch die Kraft das Wasser hebt!
Es steigt und schwindet, schwillt und schwebt,
es steht im Strahl, es kommt und fällt
in diese nasse Gotteswelt,

die zwecklos wie am ersten Tag
bloß ihrer Lust genügen mag
und von dem holden Überfluß
an keine Pflicht verstatten muß,

nur jener einen Macht sich beugt,
die sie erschuf – zum Himmel steigt
ihr Dank, ein immer, früh und spät,
unendlich rauschendes Gebet,

Das rauscht und raunt, das rinnt und rennt
im daseinsseligen Element;
es fällt empor und steigt herab –
kalt ist die Sonne, heiß das Grab.

Und da es lebt, indem es stirbt,
das Licht noch um das Wasser wirbt:
Der Geist, dem solche Lust gefiel,
dankt ihr ein Regenbogenspiel!

Ob auch die Schale überfließt,
ob Alles sich in nichts, ergießt:
der Geist, der es besieht, gewinnt,
und ob auch Lust und Zeit verrinnt.

Und nichts besteht und Alles bleibt,
dem heiligen Geiste einverleibt,
der nah dem Ursprung, treu und echt
fortlebt dem heiligen Geschlecht.

BEFORE A FOUNTAIN

Villa Torlonia

Oh how the force the water lifts!
It climbs and dwindles, swells and drifts,
it streaming stands, it falls and flows
into this wet God's world below.

that aimless, as on that first day,
but satisfy its pleasure may,
and from the lovely plenty now
need not to any duty bow,

to only that one might bends low
that brought it forth – to heaven go
its thanks, forever, early, late,
a rushing prayer, unending, great.

It rushes, murmurs, runs and flows
in stream that joy of being knows:
it falls aloft and downward climbs,
cold is the sun, the grave hot, burns.

Because it lives in that it dies,
the light still for the water vies:
The soul who liked such pleasure gay
must thank it for a rainbow's play.

E'en if the bowl should overflow,
though all things into nothing go,
the soul that views it wins the day,
though time and pleasure pass away.

And naught persists and all remains,
the holy spirit all contains,
who near the source, true, real and free
lives on for the holy family.

Der Brunnen rauscht, nur ihm vertraut
vom Jauchzen bis zum Klagelaut,
dem ewigen Ton, der ihm nur sagt,
daß hier die Lust die Welt beklagt,

die ihre Lust zum Zweck verdarb,
bis alles Licht des Lebens starb;
die sich die eigene Liebe stahl
und sich bestraft mit Scham und Qual.

Noch fließt ein Quell, noch flammt ein Licht,
noch streben beide zum Gedicht,
noch steigt die Sehnsucht hoch empor,
noch öffnet sich ein Himmelstor –

noch wär' ich auf dem Regenbogen
beinah mit dir dort eingezogen,
daß nie verrinne Lust und Zeit.
O schöne Überflüssigkeit!

The fountain's rush, to it but known
from shout of joy to grieving's tone,
the eternal sound, but bearing tale
that here our joys the world bewail,

that spoiled all joy, made it instead
and aim, til all life's light was dead;
that robbed itself its love to gain,
and scourged itself with shame and pain.

Still flows a spring, a light flames free,
still strive the both for poetry,
and longing still ascends on high,
a gate still opens in the sky –

yet would upon the rainbow too
I almost have moved in with you,
that time and joy might never flee.
O lovely superfluity!

CARL DALLAGO

SOMMERSTROPHEN

Der Sommer schüttet seine Fülle aus,
Ich bin zu Gast bei diesem Götterschmaus.
Lavendelrasen meine Liegestatt,
Ich zieh' den Duft in mich und werd' nicht satt.

Ich fühle nur, wie ich erschlossen bin,
Der Glanz des Tags berauscht mir Seel' und Sinn.
Ein Baum erhebt sein schirmendes Gezweig,
Vor solcher Guttat ich mich tief verneig.

Umrahmt von Laub und Licht wird mir so weit,
Ich bin erfüllt von Aufgeschlossenheit.
Sie weist mir Weg und Steg ins Sein hinein,
Und läßt mich Teilhaber der Schöpfung sein.

Der Schöpfung, die mir Amt und Tun bestimmt,
Die alles Leben gibt und wieder nimmt.
Mein Erdendasein ist ihr zugewandt,
So faß ich Fuß und habe festen Stand.

SUMMER STANZAS

The summer pours its fullness out abroad
And I'm a guest at this feast of the gods.
Upon a lawn of lavender I lie,
I breathe the scent, unsated yet am I.

I feel but how my soul is open wide,
The glowing day enthralls me deep inside.
A tree its shady limbs spreads over me,
I deeply bow before such charity.

Enlarged, as leaves and light around me press,
I'm filled, consumed now with receptiveness.
It points the way into true life for me,
Lets me a partner of creation be.

Creation that my station, deeds ordains,
That all life give and takes away again.
To it may life on earth I dedicate,
Thus footing gain, firm place to stand create.

LUDWIG GOLDSCHEIDER

MONATSVERSE

Januar

Wie Glas und Glocken klingt der Baum im Wind.
Das junge Jahr lacht wie ein junges Kind.
Der Schimmel trinkt, es raucht der kalte Trog,
Der Bach blieb stehen und der Traum zerrinnt.

Februar

Die Schleier, die an kalter Scheibe stehen:
Du darfst in ihnen Berg und Blume sehen
Und Antlitz wunderbar und unvergessen –
Nur atme nicht! es müßte sonst vergehen.

März

Vor blauem Himmel schwankt ein weißer Ast.
Ist weiße Blüte oder Schnee die Last?
Was brennt so froh in dir? Der alte Gram?
An dunkler Schwelle steht und staunt der Gast.

April

Nun pocht es nachts ums Dach mit hellen Hufen.
Ein Vogel schreit, die fremden Reiter rufen.
Es klopft das Herz! Der Morgen kommt! Wir steigen
Ins Blau empor auf leichten Wolkenstufen.

Mai

Die Blumen brennen wieder. Falter drängen
Um bunte Flammen, die sie nicht versengen.
Das Feuer lockt: an einem heißen Munde,
An flackernd roter Blüte blieb ich hängen.

MONTH-VERSES

January

The tree in wind rings glass-like, bell-like, gay.
The young year laughs like some young child at play.
The gray horse drinks, there smokes the frigid trough,
The brook stood still and this dream melts away.

February

The veils that stand upon the frigid pane:
You may in them see mount and blossom, plain,
And face both wonderful and unforgotten –
But do not breathe! lest it be lost again.

March

Against blue sky one sees a white branch swing.
Is blossom white or snow its burdening?
What burns so glad in you? the ancient grief?
At darkened sill the guest stands marveling.

April

Now bright hooves tap around the roof at night.
The foreign riders call, birds scream, take flight.
The heart is beating! Morning comes! We climb
Into the blue on cloud-steps soft and light.

May

The flowers burn again. The butterflies
Round colored flames unburning press and rise.
The fire entices, at a torrid mouth,
A red bloom, flaring, held me as its prize.

Juni

Das Gras fließt weich wie Haar um Frauenwangen,
Die Bäume rings voll heller Blüten prangen.
Ob du zurückkehrst oder nicht, du Liebste,
Der Duft und alles ist ja doch vergangen.

Juli

Die Luft steht dicht und schwirrt wie Fensterglas.
Die Hitze summt und atmet aus dem Gras.
Süß riecht das Heu. Versinkend höre ich
Die Stimme wieder, die ich nie vergaß.

August

Wie eine weiße Sense saust das Licht.
Verbirgst du, hoher Mäher, dein Gesicht?
Es laufen tausend Stimmen durch das Korn,
Du hinter Blau und Wolken hörst sie nicht.

September

Nun, da das Laub aus allen Kronen fällt,
Hat sich der Blick zum Himmel aufgehellt.
Vergilbte Lust! Schon strahlt mit stillem Glanz
Im Abgrund oben größer dir die Welt.

Oktober

Der Regen murmelt in der Regenrinne,
Es kräht der Wetterhahn auf seiner Zinne,
Es rollt und rollt die graue Wolkenwolle
Und immer dichter spinnt die Nebelspinne.

November

Am Tag der Toten fällt ein feiner Regen.
Gespenster drohen dir auf allen Wegen.
Wo gibt's hier eine Schenke? fragt der Wandrer
Und geht dem warmen Licht des Dorfs entgegen.

June

Like hair round ladies' cheeks soft grasses flow,
The shining, bloom-filled trees around us glow.
And whether you return or not, belovèd,
The scent and all are gone, as well you know.

July

The air stands dense and whirs like windowglass.
The hotness hums, is breathing from the grass.
The hay smells sweet. Again I sinking hear
The voice that never from my mind did pass.

August

So like a scythe of white, light whistles through.
You hide your face, High Reaper, from us too?
There run a thousand voices through the grain,
You hear them not behind the clouds and blue.

September

Now, that the leaves from all the treetops fall,
The skyward view is brightened for us all.
The yellowed joy! In that abyss above
Already softly greater shines earth's ball.

October

There in its gutter murmurs now the rain,
The weathercock crows on its crag again,
The woolly clouds of gray roll on and on,
Fogspider spins more densely in the lane.

November

On Dead-Day falls a rain that's fine and gray.
Ghosts threaten you on every path today.
Where is a tavern here? the wand'rer asks
And toward warm village light then makes his way.

Dezember

So komm doch, Schlaf! Ich wende mich zur Wand.
Nun stirbt das Jahr. Die Lust war längst verbrannt.
Frag nicht, mein Gott! Laß deine Finsternis
Auf meinen Augen ruhn, die kühle Hand.

SOMMERNACHT

Der Schläfer sinkt sanft in die Kissen hinein,
Die Lider verschließen das Angesicht.
Gelöscht ist das friedliche Abendlicht,
Aufdämmert so schön ein Schein.

Der Säugling schmatzt mit den Lippen im Traum;
Allmählich lächelt der Greis bewegt;
Die Hand auf das Herz hat das Mädchen gelegt;
An's Fenster pocht leise der Baum.

Die Nester schaukeln behutsam im Wind,
Aufzwitschern die Vögel im Traume leis
Und rühren die Flügel und sind auf der Reis'
Nach Ländern die sonniger sind.

Die Braut küßt träumend die eigene Hand
Und wird im Schlafe ganz blaß vor Glück,
Großvater findet in's Kinderland
Weinend den Weg zurück.

Im Walde verirrt, schläft traulich das Kind,
Im Grase daneben atmet das Reh.
Die Mutter wartet in Angst und Weh
Und weint sich die Augen blind.

Der Knabe steht wieder am Gartenzaun;
Düfte so hold von Hollunder wehn,
Sie lächelt gar süß im Vorübergehn
Ohne ihn auzuschaun.

December

So come then, sleep! So to the wall I turn.
Now dies the year. Joy ceased long since to burn.
Ask not, my God! Let darkness rest upon
My eyes, thus let me Thy cool hand discern.

SUMMER NIGHT

The sleeper sinks down in soft pillows and fine,
The lids close his face to the world tonight.
And quenched is the evening's peaceful light,
There dawns such a lovely shine.

While dreaming, the baby's lips smack and part;
The old man stirs slowly, smilingly;
The window is tapped by the branch of a tree;
The maiden's hand lies on her heart.

The birds' nests carefully rock in the breeze,
There twitter the birds in their dreams so soft,
And moving their wings they are gently aloft
Toward warmer and sunnier leas.

The bride's lips dreamily kiss her own hand
And in her sleep she grows pale with joy,
Grandfather, weeping, re-finds the land
Where he was once a boy.

While lost in the woods, a child snugly sleeps,
Nearby in the grass stands breathing a deer.
The mother waits now in grief and fear,
Her eyes blind with tears, she weeps.

The boy near the garden fence takes his stance;
Fragrance blows sweet from the elders nigh,
She smiles very sweetly in passing by,
Giving him not a glance.

Der Landstreicher schnarcht auf dem warmen Mist,
Zitternd verbeugt sich vor ihn der Gendarm.
Elisabeth schläft, ihr Püppchen im Arm,
Das lebendig geworden ist.

Vom Winde gerüttelt das Fenster klirrt,
Auf den Gläsern liegt ein silberner Schein.
Der Dichter steht am Fenster allein,
Und flüstert und lächelt verwirrt.

Und der Dichter hört, wie die Zweige sich drehn,
Wie das Wasser geheim in der Traufe rauscht;
Und schauernd schließt er die Augen und lauscht
Und weiß nicht wie ihm geschehn.

Und der Dichter spricht: ,,O traumgrüne Welt,
Ich hab dich so lieb, ich bin dir so gut!
Wie der Strom in's Meer, strömt in dich mein Blut.
Nun ist es so selig geschwellt.''

Die Vögel seufzen im Traume leis,
Die Wipfel sausen so nah und so fern.
Durch's schwankende Laub hin senden die Stern'
Strahlen so fein und weiß.

Der Dichter spricht: ,,Nun träumen sie tief,
O, daß ich aus Träumen nach Hause fänd'!
Ich darf noch nicht schlafen, erst muß ich zu End'
Schreiben an Gott den Brief.''

And on the warm dung the tramp snores, content,
Trembling, the gendarme bends down to him there.
Asleep, in her arms Elizabeth fair
Holds a doll to which life is lent.

The window is rattled by night wind while
On the glasses glows a silvery tone.
The poet stands at the window alone,
Bewildered he whispers, his smile.

And the poet hears the soft dance of each limb,
How the water-filled gutter sighs secretly;
With shudders, eyes closed, he listens, and he
Knows not what's been done to him.

And the poet speaks: "O dreamy green land,
I love you so much, o I care, I do!
As the stream to the sea, streams my blood into you.
How blissfully did it expand."

The birds sigh softly in dreams tonight,
The branches sough now so near, so far.
Through wavering leaves sends many a star
Lightrays so fine and white.

The poet speaks: "In deep dreams they nod,
O, if I could only send home from dreams!
I may not yet slumber, first must I, it seems,
Write this letter to God."

GESPRÄCH MIT DEM MOND

Stille lieg ich, sinnend, traumentrissen,
Weißes Mondlicht spielt auf weißen Kissen.

„Mond, du darfst mit deinem Licht nicht prahlen!
Von der Sonne hast du deine Strahlen."

„—Ja, von ihr hab ich mein Licht empfangen,
Und es glänzt nur bis sie aufgegangen.

„Schimmern denn nicht Träume und Gedichte
So von Leben, einem fernen Lichte?

„Wird denn nicht auch wiederum dem Leben
Licht von einem größern Licht gegeben?

„Sind die Strahlen, die dein Herz durchfluten,
Nicht ein Wiederschein der ew'gen Gluten?

Geht die Sonne auf, muß ich vergehen
Neues Leben sang ich ungesehen.

„Höhern Lichtes Aufgang und Entbrennen
Magst du 'Tod,' – ich will es 'Morgen' nennen."

Stille lieg ich, sinnend, traumentrissen:
Weißes Mondlicht spielt auf weißen Kissen.

CONVERSATION WITH THE MOON

I lie quiet, musing, torn from dreams,
O'er white pillows whitest moonlight streams.

"Moon, you may not boast of your own light!
From the sun you have your rays so white."

" '–Yes, from her I have my light so fair,
And it glows but til she's risen there.

" 'Do not dreams and poems also shimmer
Thus from life, a strong yet distant glimmer?

" 'Is not life then given in return,
Light from where a greater light must burn?

" 'Are the rays that through your heart now flow
Not reflected from eternal glow?

" 'When the sun comes up, I pass away,
Draw new life while unseen I must stay.

" 'Higher light's new rising, all in flame –
"Death" for you – for me bears "Morning's" name.' "

I lie quiet, musing, torn of dreams:
O'er white pillows whitest moonlight streams.

IDA SCHWARZ

AN EINE WOLKE

Eine aus dem großen Volke,
leichte, schwanenweiße Wolke,
schwebst du hinterm Berg herauf.
Und, befreit von eigner Schwere,
über Länder, über Meere,
folgen andre dir zuhauf.

Kommend aus entrückter Ferne,
denkst du schon der vielen Sterne,
da die Sonne untergeht.
Wind, dein ungestümer Freier,
flieht mit dir des Himmels Feuer,
eh das All in Flammen steht.

Die dir folgten, goldumrandet,
sind auf halbem Weg gestrandet.
Durch die Bläue eilest du,
wie auf unsichtbarem Flügel,
über Täler, über Hügel,
nahem Horizonte zu.

TO A CLOUD

One of a much larger crowd,
light and fleecy swan-white cloud,
you behind the mountain rise.
And of their own weight now free
over land and over sea
others follow through the skies.

Coming from a distance far,
you think of the many stars,
when the dark the sunlight claims.
Wind, your suitor, stormy, yearning,
flees with you from heaven's burning
ere the cosmos stands in flames.

Those who followed, goldenbanded,
half way there are lying stranded.
Through the heavens, azure, fine,
as on unseen wings you hurry,
over hills and valleys scurry
to the near horizon line.

OTTO STOESSL

MONDFABEL

Mond muß frieren bei der Nacht,
„Mutter hat kein Kleid gebracht,
Mutter soll mir eines nähen,
Daß ich unter Leute gehen,
Warm es haben kann bei Nacht."
„Keiner hat mir Zeug gebracht,
Soll ich Wollewolken fassen?
Nie wird Dir ein Röckchen passen,
Heute bist Du kugelrund,
Morgen dünner, sichelschmal
Und bist manches liebe Mal
Gar in nichts vergangen.
Heute klein und morgen groß
Mußt Du schon so nackt und bloß
Zwischen Erd und Himmel hangen."

MOON FABLE

Moon must freeze up there at night,
"Mother brought no dresses bright,
Mother should sew one for me,
That I may with people be,
Have it soft and warm at night."
  "None has brought me fabric bright,
Should I grasp wool-clouds, a few?
Never will a skirt fit you,
You today are spherical,
Slim tomorrow, crescent-spare
And so often have you there
Vanished quite away.
Small today, tomorrow great,
Naked, bare, so must you wait,
There 'tween earth and heaven stay."

JOSEF WEINHEBER

IM GRASE

Glocken und Zyanen,
Thymian und Mohn.
Ach, ein fernes Ahnen
hat das Herz davon.

Seh die Schiffe ziehen,
fühl den Wellenschlag,
weiße Wolken fliehen
durch den späten Tag –

Glocken und Zyanen,
Mohn und Thymian.
Himmlisch wehn die Fahnen
über grünem Plan:

Und im sanften Nachen
trägt es so dahin.
Zwischen Traum und Wachen
frag ich, wo ich bin.

Löwenzahn und Raden,
Klee und Rosmarin.
Lenk es, Gott, in Gnaden
nach der Heimat hin.

Das is deine Stille.
Ja, ich hör dich schon.
Salbei und Kamille,
Thymian und Mohn,

und schon halb im Schlafen
– Mohn und Thymian –
landet sacht im Hafen
nun der Nachen an.

IN THE GRASS

Blue cyanus growing,
Poppies, thyme and bells.
Far, an almost-knowing
In the heart now swells.

Moving ships I'm seeing,
Feeling billows play,
Clouds of white are fleeing
Through the long late day.

Blue cyanus growing,
Poppies, thyme and bells.
Flags are grandly blowing
O'er green plains and dells:

Thither thus it's taking
In the gentle pram.
And 'mid dream and waking
I ask where I am.

Dandelions, clover,
Rosemary and weed.
God, in grace it over
To the homeland lead.

I hear you already.
There's your quiet time.
Camomile so heady,
Poppy, sage and thyme.

And now halfway sleeping
– Poppy, thyme again –
Landward softly creeping,
Boat does harbor gain.

ARTHUR ZANKER

HOCHZEITSSONETT

Neues Leben soll beginnen
zwischen Reigen und Chorälen.
Denn es gilt den Weg zu wählen
zwischen Gott und unseren Sinnen.

Möge wilder Mohn sich einen
mit der stillen Glut am Herde.
Heilig sollen Brot und Erde
uns von heute an erscheinen.

Und das Glas, daraus wir trinken,
wollen wir in Ruhe heben,
mit der Rechten und der Linken.

So mit beiden Händen halten,
so Gebet und Trunk verweben,
Händegriff und Händefalten.

GROSSELTERNHAUS

Des großen Bauernhauses säuerliche Kühle,
der Schritte Hallen in den weiten Fluren,
das Pendeln und der Klang der alten Uhren,
die breiten Bänke und die steilen Stühle.

Die rohen Balken an der Zimmerdecke,
der Duft gebackenen Brotes in den Öfen,
der scharfe Stallgeruch ... Und in den Höfen
für uns, die Kinder, herrliche Verstecke.

Am Boden reifes Obst, im Keller Weine
und Schnaps, gebrannt aus Pflaumen und Wacholder.
Erinnerung bewahrt mir immer holder
den Duft der fernen Zeit, der Kindheit Reine.

WEDDING SONNET

This be where new life commences
'Mid chorale and roundelay.
For we have to choose the way
Now between God and our senses.

Let us join wild poppy here
With the still glow of our hearth.
Holy shall both bread and earth
From this day to us appear.

And the glass from which we drink,
Let us lift in peace the wine
With the right and left, and think.

So with both hands let us grasp,
So our prayer and drink entwine,
Handshake and hands' prayerful clasp.

GRANDPARENTS' HOUSE

The frangrance of the large old farmhouse cool and sour,
the clang of footsteps in wide vestibules,
the benches broad, the straight-backed chairs, the stools,
the sounds of ancient clocks that strike the hour.

On chamber ceiling, rough-hewn beams and braces,
from ovens, fresh bread's smell upon the air,
the acrid scent of barn . . . And in yards there
for us, the children, wondrous hiding places.

Ripe fallen fruit, and in the cellar wines
and gin distilled from plums and juniper.
My memory keeps ever lovelier
the scent of distant childhood's pure designs.

Und hinter alledem die nackte Erde,
auf brauner Ackerscholle Roßgeschnaube,
Großvaters Schritt am Pflug und fester Glaube,
den ich im Blute nie verlieren werde.

And there behind all that the naked ground,
on brown field-soil the work horse pants along,
grandfather at the plow, faith firm and strong
that in my blood forever will abound.

JOSEPH GEORG OBERKOFLER

DER ERBE

Knabe, du kamst nicht allein
In das Haus am Birkenrain.
Als die Wiege dich empfing,
Durch den weiten Friedhof ging
Mächtig deiner Ahnen Schritt
Und sie alle gingen mit.

Treten wirst du ihnen gleich
In ihr altes Bauernreich.
Kreuz, Gerät und Ackerland
Wächst dir zu aus ihrer Hand.
Schön ist Haus und Hof bestellt,
Schild und Wehr für deine Welt.

Knecht und Dirnen jung und stark
Gehn durch die besonnte Mark.
Brunnen rauscht und Mühle geht.
Iß und trink und schaff und bet.
Blüten treibt der Stamm gesund
Neu auf deinem Frühlingsgrund.

Knabe, du kommst nicht allein
Einst ins Grab am Kirchenrain.
Wenn der Sarg dich stumm empfängt,
Wogend in die Kammer drängt
Mächtig deiner Ahnen Schritt,
Und sie alle gehen mit.

THE HEIR

Not alone you came, boy, no,
To the house near yon birch row.
As the cradle welcomed you
Through the spacious graveyard too
Went your fathers' mighty stride,
With you they all came inside.

Like them you will enter bold
This their peasant kingdom old.
Cross and tools and farming land
You inherit from their hand.
Ordered well are house and field,
For your world, defense and shield.

Farmhands, maids, strong, young and good,
Wander through the sunlit wood.
Mill goes round, springs murmur gay,
Eat and drink and work and pray.
Stems send blossoms, healthy, sound,
New upon your cool spring ground.

Boy, alone you will not go
To your churchyard grave, ah, no!
When the coffin welcomes you,
Strong into the chamber too
Surging, will your fathers' stride
Press, and they'll go at your side.

ALMA JOHANNA KOENIG

TRAURIGE ODE

Einsam bin ich. Es wob mir die spinnende Parze
Keinen Faden, dem andre sich goldig verflechten,
Nein, er flattert haltlos, wie sonnenbeglänztes
                Spinnwerk des Herbstes.

Einsam bleib' ich. Es ward mir kein Häuschen gefüget,
Bunt von Blumen. Kein Herd mir vom Gatten errichtet.
Keines Kindes Gelalle grüßt mich und rufet der Mutter,
                ach, keines Kindes!

Müde treib' ich hinab den Strom meines Lebens,
Rühre die Ruder nicht mehr. Wohin mich auch immer
Strömung treibt, oder Wind, oder Götterbeschließung,
                ich will's erdulden.

Ruhiger rauscht schon der Fluß und rauscht die rinnende Welle
Meines brausenden Bluts. Schon seh' ich neblige Wiesen,
Treibend streift Zweige mein Boot und unter hängende Weiden
                neig' ich den Scheitel . . .

SAD ODE

Lonely I am. There wove me the destiny spinning
Not a thread with which others weave golden together,
No, it flutters loosely, like sunnily glowing
                    spinwork of autumn.

Lonely I stay. For me was not built here a cottage
Bright with flowers. No hearth by a husband erected.
And no babble of children greets me and calls to the mother
                    ah, of no children!

Weary, I drive on down my life's flowing river,
Touching the paddles no more. I'm drifting wherever
Drives me the current or wind, or the gods' resolution,
                    I will endure it.

Stiller now rushes the river, sighs the onrunning wave of
My impetuous blood. Now I see misty soft meadows,
Driving, my boat brushes twigs and under pendulous willows
                    my head I lower . . .

CREDO

Es ist mein Amt nicht zu vermaledei'n.
Zum Trost berufen, aber nicht zum Fluche,
ist es mein armes Teil, wenn ich versuche,
im allerengsten Rahmen gut zu sein.

Was auch an Leiden die Geschichte buche,
den großen Sündern möge Gott verzeih'n. –
Ich zeichne an des Bildes Rand mich ein,
mit seinem Inhalt stumm im Widerspruche.

Denn wie der Sperling ohne Unterlaß
im Abfall pickend seine Nahrung findet,
so such' auch ich in einer Welt voll Haß

nach Liebe, die uns tiefgeheim verbindet.
Und davon leb' ich, – mich erhält nur das:
Ich liebe, – und wer liebt, der überwindet.

WHAT I BELIEVE

To curse is not the office given me.
To comfort called, but not to imprecation,
'tis my poor lot, when I with concentration
try in life's tightest framework good to be.

What history records of tribulation,
may God forgive great sinners graciously. –
I sign the picture's edge reluctantly,
though mute in conflict with its implication.

For as the sparrow pecking e'er again
in refuse there its nourishment will find,
so seek I in a world of hate and pain

just love that in deep secret us does bind.
From that I live, – just that does me sustain:
I love – who loves prevails, life's so designed.

EUGENIE FINK

LEBENSDANK

Daß ich dieses klare Morgenschweigen,
angelehnt an birkenhelle Rinde,
mit dem Blick auf Ähren, die sich neigen,
wie Gesang und wie ein Glück empfinde,
dank ich dir auf festlich stillen Wegen.
Eine Seele, die von Demut weiß,
neigt sich tief vor deinem Erntesegen,
eingeschlossen in der Schöpfung Kreis.

GRATITUDE TO LIFE

That I revel in this clear dawn stillness,
Leaning on the birch bark brightly gleaming,
Gazing o'er the corn that sways so listless,
Like a song, like some good fortune feeling,
Thanks I bear to you in festive calmness.
Soul that knows humility of mind,
Lowly bows before your harvest's richness,
All within creation's sphere confined.

HERBERT STRUTZ

MÄRZNACHT

Der Atem Gottes sank auf braches Land
und tauchte in der Wurzeln harte Knoten.
Da brach ein Blütenwogen aus den toten
Lenzäckern und entfachte wilden Brand.

Der Himmel lag voll Leuchten ausgespannt
und seltne Wolken, frühe Sturmesboten,
versprachen Regen, während aus den roten
Glurändern schon der bleiche Nachttrabant

aufwuchs. Er hing wie eine reife Beere
im Sterngestrüpp, das seine blanken Dolden
verstreut ins weiche Dunkel sinken ließ.

Und wie in hartem Sturz, so sank der schwere
und weite Himmel in mein Schauen, golden
verzaubernd Welt und Raum zum Paradies.

MARCH NIGHT

The breath of God sank down on fallow land,
into the roots' hard knots 'twas diving led.
Then broke a wave of blossoms from the dead
spring farmlands and wild fire it kindled, fanned.

The sky lay full, with lights across it spanned,
strange clouds, storm's early heralds, thunderheads
gave pledge of showers, rain, while from the red
glow's edge already night's pale footman grand

arose. It like a berry ripe did hang
in starry bush, that let its umbels bright
sink strewn into the darkness softly curled.

And as when falling hard, the heavens sank,
the broad and heavy sky into my sight,
to paradise enchanting space and world.

EIN BAUERNSOHN SCHREIBT AUS DER STADT

Mein lieber Vater! Während ich dies schreibe,
denk ich nach Haus. War wohl die Ernte gut?
Du willst, daß ich noch in der Fremde bleibe.
Wenn du nur wüßtest, Vater, wie das tut!

Ich träume viel vom Dorf, vom Hof, von allen
den guten Dingen, die man hier nicht kennt.
Und lausche oft: Ob jetzt die Harken schallen?
Und ob das Hirtenfeuer abends brennt?

Denn weißt du wohl: Vor kurzem saß ich selber
noch auf der Weide; und ich sann ins Land,
indes der Abendhimmel als ein gelber
und riesengroßer Brand darüber stand.

Und dann trieb ich im Dunkel Roß und Kühe
zur Tränke und zum Stall. Feucht war das Gras . . .
Doch jetzt, ach, Vater! Sieh, ich geb mir Mühe
mit all den Büchern. Aber nützt das was?

Du schreibst: du willst, daß ich recht tüchtig werde.
Kein Bauer, sondern . . . Das sei harte Fron . . .
Begreifst du es denn nicht: mir fehlt die Erde.
Die Erde, Vater! – Lebewohl. Dein Sohn.

A FARMER'S SON WRITES FROM THE CITY

My dearest Father! As I write today,
I think of home. Was harvest good to you?
Your will is that I still abroad should stay.
Oh, Father, what that does, if you but knew!

I dream of village, farm and everything,
Of all the goodness that they here don't know.
And listen often: Do the rakes now ring?
And does the shepherd's fire at evening glow?

For well you know: Not long ago still I
Sat on the field and thought into the land,
The while all yellow there the evening sky
A great enormous flame did o'er it stand.

In darkness drove I horse and cattle there
To water, to the stall. The grass was wet . . .
But now, oh, Father! See, I take great care
With all the books. But is there use in that?

You write, you want me capable to be.
No farmer, rather . . . That's hard work, not fun . . .
Do you not grasp: I miss the earth, you see.
The earth, my Father! – Now farewell. Your son.

HANS LEIFHELM

WINTERWALD

Ich geh in einen Winterwald hinein,
Der Winterwald muß voller Wunder sein.

Die Tannen stehen enge angeschmiegt,
Soweit das Land in tiefer Schneelast liegt.

Und keine Spuren gehen durch den Wald
Als vom Getier – und die verwehen bald.

Und manchmal ist ein Seufzen in den Bäumen
Wie Kinder seufzen unter tiefen Träumen.

Der Schnee liegt weiß so weit ich wandern will,
Da werden alle Menschenwünsche still.

HERBSTLICHER RUF

Komm mit, verlaß die Tenne und die Kelter,
Es schwelt ein bittrer Duft in Herbstessüße,
Laß rauschen durch das welke Laub die Füße,
Es rinnt das Stundenglas, die Welt wird älter.

In Herbstessüße schwelt ein bittrer Duft,
Der Sommer geht, das Alte muß verderben,
Sieh wie die Ähren und die Wipfel sterben,
Versehrend haucht die Kühle durch die Luft.

Die Füße rauschen durch das welke Laub –
O Herz, entreiße dich den Herbstgesängen,
Sieh wie die Kätzchen an den Haseln drängen,
Sie bergen schon der neuen Zeugung Staub.

WINTER FOREST

I walk into a forest wintery,
The winter woods must full of wonders be.

The pine trees snuggled close together stand
As far as 'neath snow's burden lies the land.

And through the forest go no tracks today
But those of deer – soon blown away.

And often in the trees there is a sighing,
As children sigh when 'neath deep dreams they're lying.

The snow lies white as far as I would go,
And there all human wishes silent grow.

AUTUMN CALL

Come on, let threshing-floor and winepress stand!
A bitter scent in autumn sweetness smoulders,
Let rustle feet where withered foliage moulders,
The world grows older, th'hourglass drops its sand.

Scent bitter burns in autumn sweet and fair,
The old must spoil, the summer goes a-flying,
See how the ears and treetops now are dying,
The coolness whispers wounding through the air.

The footsteps rustle through the withered leaves –
O spirit, tear yourself from autumn's singing,
See how the squirrels to the nuts are springing,
They hide the dust of what anew conceives.

Es rinnt das Stundenglas, komm mit und schau,
Es reift der Same rings in jeder Frucht,
Die Wolken harren trächtig in der Bucht,
Auf weißem Zelter kommt die Winterfrau.

Komm mit, verlaß die Kelter und die Tenne,
Es schwelt ein neuer Duft in Herbstessüße,
Laß rauschen durch das welke Laub die Füße,
Befiehl dem Herzen, daß es neu entbrenne.

LOB DER VERGÄNGLICHKEIT

So will ich dich preisen, Vergänglichkeit, die du beherrschest die irdische Zeit,
Die du das Leben inbrünstiger machst, die du auch flammender mich entfachst,
Kündend die Nimmerwiederkehr, kündend das eherne Nimmermehr.

Einmal und einzig ist jedes Geschehn, nicht wird die Welle als gleiche erstehn,
Die sich zu meinen Füßen bricht, einmal wird Jedes geboren zum Licht,
Während sich rings schon der Schatten schart, während Geburt mit dem Tode sich paart.

Inbrunst sei dir flammend geweckt, – sieh das kleine glaszarte Insekt,
Das beim Anhauch flüchtig entschwebt, auch in diesem Vergänglichsten lebt
Schönheit des Einzigen unversehrt, die dir nimmermehr wiederkehrt.

Leben ist Sterben immerdar, aber einzig und wunderbar
Jedes Geschehen dem Dunkel entbricht, jedes Leben auffunkelt im Licht,
In der Einmaligkeit hochgeweiht, unversehrbar in irdischer Zeit.

Dunkel liegt deine Zukunft verdeckt, Inbrunst sei dir flammend geweckt,
Nichts im Handeln eitel zu tun, nicht in der Träge Schatten zu ruhn,
Uns ist verliehen der Liebenden Kraft und des Wahrhaftigen Leidenschaft.

The hourglass runs, come with and share the sight,
The seed grows ripe in every fruit today,
The clouds are waiting pregnant o'er the bay,
The winter woman comes on horse of white.

Come on, let threshing-floor and winepress stand!
A fragrance new in autumn sweetness smoulders,
Let rustle feet where withered foliage moulders,
To burn anew with love the heart command.

PRAISE OF TRANSITORINESS

Thus you will I praise now, o transiency, you who earth's time hold in mastery,
You who make life much more ardent and bright, you who more fervently me excite,
Saying all's gone that's been before, saying naught will return evermore.

Once and once only comes every event, never again will the same wave be sent
That now is breaking at my feet, only in one birth does each the light greet,
While all around shadows gather there, while birth and death form together a pair.

Let warm ardour flame up for you, – see the fragile small insect now too
That a breath drives floating away, also has here this most fleeting day
Beauty undamaged, unique, in store, which returns to you nevermore.

Living will always dying be, and yet unique and wondrously
Every event still breaks forth from the night, every life scintilates in the light,
In its uniqueness sacred, sublime, free from harm in terrestrial time.

Darkly your future's hidden from view, let warm ardour flame up for you,
Naught in action vainly to test, nor in the shadow of sloth to rest,
Life us with power of lovers did bless and gave us passion of truthfulness.

Leben ist Sterben immerdar, aber lebendig im späteren Jahr
Macht es die Regung unserer Brust, denn des Ewigen währende Lust
Wirft schon Abglanz in unser Herz, jedes Geschehen schreibt sich in Erz.

Gutes und Böses wirkt weiter fort, so wie das Licht, so strahlt auch das Wort,
Strahlt auch die flüchtigste Regung des Hirns über die Bahnen unsres Gestirns,
Untilgbar in der Sternenbahn wirkt was getan, was nicht getan.

Einmal der Mensch und nur einmal der Tag, denk es bei jedem Herzensschlag,
Nichts, was geschieht wird nichtig gemacht, nichts was versäumt, wird später vollbracht,
Jeder wahre sein heiliges Recht, jeder verbürge des anderen Recht!

VOM HOFFENDEN LEBEN

Beim Schmelzen des Schnees, bei den lauen
Lüften des Februar
Wollen wir wieder vertrauen
Auf das grünende Jahr,
Sieh, den Amseln, den kleinen,
Schwillt das singende Herz,
Und an den nackten Rainen
Glänzt die Scholle wie Erz.

Schau des Landmanns Beginnen
Der Schnee um den Obstbaum häuft,
Daß nicht zu früh nach innen
Lösend das Tauwasser träuft,
Daß nicht aus ruhendem Schweigen
Aufbricht, was nicht gedeiht,
Und die Säfte nicht steigen
In der gefährdeten Zeit.

Living is always dying here, but our breast's stirring in some later year
Gives it the life that it may require, for th' Eternal One's lasting desire
Casts reflection in our heart's glass, every event is written in brass.

Good things and evil work undeterred, as does the light so beams too the word,
Beams the mind's fleetingest stirring afar, out o'er the orbits of our own stars,
Imprinted in the starry way, what's done or not will e'er bear sway.

Man is but once and but once is the day, reflect as each heartbeat is fading away,
Naught that occurs is nullified, vain, naught that was missed can we ever regain,
Let each one safeguard his holy rights, let each one vouch for his fellowman's rights!

ON THE HOPING LIFE

At the melting of snow, February
Breezes so mild and clear,
Let's in us faith again carry
In the green-growing year,
See, with song swell o'erflowing
Hearts of small blackbirds there,
And the soil like brass glowing
On the boundaries bare.

See the farmer's beginning,
Who snow round the fruit tree heaps,
That not too early winning
Inward the meltwater seeps,
That not from silence there sleeping
Bursts forth what cannot flower,
That not upward be creeping
Sap in the dangerous hour.

Also ward auch gegeben
Allem das Werdegebot,
Also muß auch das Leben
Warten auf seinen Tod,
Samen, Knospen und Blüten,
Jedes kommt und vergeht,
Uns ist geboten zu hüten,
Was in der Hoffnung steht.

Nichts ist auf Erden verloren,
Was wir dem Leben getan,
Darum sind wir geboren,
Daß wir auf unserer Bahn
Dienen dem hoffenden Leben
Zu des Gestirnes Ruhm,
Das uns zu Lehen gegeben,
Doch nicht zu Eigentum.

Thus to all was the giving
Of that commandment to grow,
Thus too must all that's living
Wait then its death to know,
Seeds and buds, blossoms bearing,
Each one comes and then dies,
We are all changed with the caring
For what in hope may rise.

Naught is on earth lost forever
That we for life do today,
To that end are we ever
Born, so that we on our way
Serve hoping life while we live it
To the stars' fame, their renown;
Life – God in fief does us give it,
But it is not our own.

FRANZ GRILLPARZER

LOB ÖSTERREICHS

O nehmt euch sein, nehmt euch des Landes an!
Er ist ein guter Herr, es ist ein gutes Land,
Wohl wert, daß sich ein Fürst sein unterwinde!
Wo habt ihr dessengleichen schon gesehn?
Schaut rings umher, wohin der Blick sich wendet,
Lachts wie dem Bräutigam die Braut entgegen!
Mit hellem Wiesengrün und Saatengold,
Von Lein und Safran gelb und blau gestickt,
Von Blumen süß durchwürzt und edlem Kraut,
Schweift es in breitgestreckten Tälern hin –
Ein voller Blumenstrauß, soweit es reicht,
Vom Silberband der Donau rings umwunden! –
Hebt sichs empor zu Hügeln voller Wein,
Wo auf und auf die goldne Traube hängt
Und schwellend reift in Gottes Sonnenglanze;
Der dunkle Wald voll Jagdlust krönt das Ganze.
Und Gottes lauer Hauch schwebt drüber hin,
Und wärmt und reift, und macht die Pulse schlagen,
Wie nie ein Puls auf kalten Steppen schlägt.
Drum ist der Österreicher froh und frank,
Trägt seinen Fehl, trägt offen seine Freuden,
Beneidet nicht, *läßt* lieber sich beneiden!
Und was er tut, ist frohen Muts getan.
's ist möglich, daß in Sachsen und beim Rhein
Es Leute gibt, die mehr in Büchern lasen;
Allein, was nottut und was Gott gefällt,
Der klare Blick, der offne, richtge Sinn,
Da tritt der Österreicher hin vor jeden,
Denkt sich sein Teil und läßt die andern reden!

O gutes Land! o Vaterland! Inmitten
Dem Kind Italien und dem Manne Deutschland,
Liegst du, der wangenrote Jüngling, da:
Erhalte Gott dir deinen Jugendsinn,
Und mache gut, was andere verdarben!

IN PRAISE OF AUSTRIA

O do support him, do support the land!
He is a goodly lord, the country too is good,
Well worthy, that a prince devote himself to it!
Where have you seen its equal heretofore?
Then look around, where'er you turn your gazing,
Like bride to bridegroom, everything is smiling!
With shining meadow-green and golden grain,
By flax and saffron blue and yellow stitched,
By blossoms sweetly spiced and precious herbs,
In broadly stretching valleys it rolls on –
A full bouquet as far as it extends,
Encircled by the silver band, the Danube! –
It lifts itself to hillsides full of vines,
Where up and up there hangs the golden grape
That in God's sunshine swells, a rip'ning treasure;
All crownded by dark woods full of hunting pleasure.
And o'er it mildly floats God's gentle breath,
And warms and ripens, sending pulses beating,
As never pulses beat upon cold plains.
The Austrian is therefore glad and free,
He bears his fault, bears openly his gladness,
Lacks envy, rather lets himself be envied!
And what he does is in good humor done.
Perhaps in Saxony and near the Rhine
Are people who more books have read or studied,
Yet in what's needed and what pleases God,
The clear glance and the mind that's open, right,
In front of all an Austrian would walk,
Would speak his mind and let the others talk!

O goodly land! o Fatherland! 'tween the two,
Child Italy and Germany, the man,
You lie, the red-cheeked adolescent, there:
May God preserve for you your sense of youth,
And make aright, what others may have ruined!

ANTON WILDGANS

ÖSTERREICHISCHES LIED

Wo sich der ewig Schnee
spiegelt im Alpensee,
Sturzbach am Fels zerstäubt,
eingedämmt Werke treibt,
wo in der Berge Herz
dämmert das Eisenerz,
Hammer Gestein zerstampft,
zischend die Schmelzglut dampft,
wo durch der Ebene Gold
silbern der Strom hinrollt,
Ufer von Früchten schwillt,
hügelan Rebe quillt,
wurzelhell, Kraft im Mark,
pflichtgewillt, duldenstark,
einfach und echt von Wort
wohnen die Menschen dort.
Pflügerschweiß, Städtefleiß
hat da die rechte Weis',
was auch Geschick beschied,
immer noch blüht ein Lied.
Österreich heißt das Land!
Da er's mit gnädiger Hand
schuf und so reich begabt,
Gott hat es lieb gehabt!

AUSTRIAN SONG

Where the eternal snow
mirrors in lake below,
stream on rock spraying spills,
dammed, drives machines and mills,
where in the mountains' core
glimmers the iron-ore
hammers stone pulverize,
fumes from the smelt-fires rise,
where through plain's golden gleam
silvery rolls the stream,
shore with the harvest swells,
hillward the vinyard wells,
root-sound, with hardiness,
dutiful, strong 'neath stress,
simple, in word sincere
people are dwelling here.
City toil, plowman's sweat,
properly here are met,
whate'er fate's brought along,
still blossoms forth a song.
Austria is the land!
Since He with gracious hand
made it, endowed it so,
God for it love did show!

PAULA VON PRERADOVIĆ

LAND DER BERGE, LAND AM STROME

Land der Berge, Land am Strome,
Land der Äcker, Land der Dome,
Land der Hämmer, zukunftsreich!
Heimat bist du großer Söhne,
Volk, begnadet für das Schöne,
Vielgerühmtes Österreich!

Heiß umfehdet, wild umstritten
Liegst dem Erdteil du inmitten,
Einem starken Herzen gleich.
Hast seit frühen Ahnentagen
Hoher Sendung Last getragen,
Vielgeprüftes Österreich!

Mutig in die neuen Zeiten,
Frei und gläubig sieh uns schreiten,
Arbeitsfroh und hoffnungsreich.
Einig laß in Brüderchören,
Vaterland, dir Treue schwören,
Vielgeliebtes Osterreich!

LAND OF MOUNTAINS, RIVERLAND

Land of mountains, riverland,
Farmland, land where churches stand,
Hammer land, of future full!
Homeland of great sons are you,
Nation, blessed for beauty too,
Austria so glory full!

Cause of feuds, strife wild and heated,
Here in Europe's center seated
Like a healthy heart and strong.
From the early days of yore
You high mission's burden bore,
Austria, tried, tested long!

Into this new era see
Us now march, brave, pious, free,
Happy workers, hopeful; and
One in brotherhood, to you
Let us swear that we'll be true,
Austria, belovéd land!

FERDINAND VON SAAR

ZWEITE WIENER ELEGIE

Ja, ich sehe dich jetzt, wie du im Schmucke des Frühlings
   weithin leuchtend dich dehnst, herrlicher Schönheit bewußt.
Einzig bist du fürwahr! Wer zählt die ragenden Bauten,
   die sich schließen zum Ring, edel und prächtig zugleich?
Hier, ein steinern Juwel, der jüngste der Dome; zum Himmel
   strebt des Doppelgetürms zierliches Stabwerk hinan;
dort, breitfrontig, mit ernsten Arkaden das mächtige Rathaus –
   und, quadrigengekrönt, attisches Marmorgebälk.
Hochweg träumen im Äther die Kuppeln der beiden Museen,
   während sich reizvoll verjüngt Habsburgs ehrwürdiges Heim.
Und so setzt es sich fort in der Runde, nur lieblich durchbrochen
   von zartfunkelndem Grün offenen Gartengehegs.
Wahrlich, ein Bild, entzückend zu schaun für jeden Betrachter,
   welchem Land er entstammt, freudig bewundert er hier;
gerne vergißt der Hesperier selbst die klassische Heimat –
   und an der wärmeren Pracht bricht sich der nordische Stolz.

SECOND VIENNESE ELEGY

Yes, I look at you now, as you in jewels of springtime
    glowing stretch yourself wide, conscious of beauty so grand.
You are unique indeed! Who counts the towering buildings
    that are forming the Ring, noble and splendid in one?
Here, a gem made of stone, the newest cathedral; the graceful
    ribs of the double tower reaching up to the sky;
there, broad-fronted, with sober arcades the magnificent town-hall –
    and, with chariots crowned, marbel Athenian beams.
High away in the ether there dream two museums' cupolas,
    while full of charm is made young Habsburg's venerable home.
It continues thus forth in a circle, so lovely, pierced only
    by soft glistening green of open garden preserve.
Truly, a sight, enchanting to see for every observer,
    from whate'er land he comes, joyful he here all admires;
gladly forgets the Hesperian e'en the classical homeland –
    and on the warmer array shatters the Nordic man's pride.

HANS JUST

NÄCHTLICHER GANG DURCH DIE BURG

Michaelerplatz in tiefer Nacht,
rings umsäumt von traumlos tiefem Schlaf.
Nur die Ordnungslichter halten Wacht,
unentwegte Wächter gelb und brav.
In den immer wachen Korridor
trete ich durchs Michaelertor.

Sporenklirrend kommt der eigne Schritt
aus barocker Wölbung Widerhall
als mein größerer Begleiter mit –
Roßgewieher und Trompetenschall.
Eh noch das Gesicht Gestalt gewann,
weht mich schon des Burghofs Halbschlaf an:

Aus dem Graben dämmerdunkeltief
steigt der Geist der Renaissance empor
und den Schweizerhof, der längst entschlief,
ahn' ich durch das dunkle Schweizertor.
Leis' umschmeicheln Früh- und Hochbarock
schwisterlich den altergrauen Block.

Bürgerlicher sich ein Bild entrollt –
Läden links und rechts von Tor zu Tor –
in des weiland Kaiser Leopold
weit geducktem Trakt und Korridor.
Dann durch dunkler Pfeiler düstre Wacht
tret' ich wieder in die schwarze Nacht.

Links die Neue Burg steht fremd und fern.
Prinz Eugens gefrorner Schatten starrt
schwarz hinan. Am Himmel nicht ein Stern.
Ob der bronzne Reiter ihn erharrt?
Ungehemmt heult hier der Wintersturm.
Eulenäugig glotzt die Zeit vom Turm.

NIGHT WALK THROUGH THE BURG

St. Michael's Square in night so deep,
hemmed around by dreamless sleep profound.
Only safety lamps a vigil keep,
yellow, worthy watchmen firm and sound.
In the always wakeful corridor
I step through the stately Michael's Door.

With the clank of spurs I hear my stride
from baroque vault cambers echoing
as a large companion at my side –
horse's neighing and a trumpet's ring.
Yet ere I the face's form can see,
comes the courtyard's half-sleep over me.

From the Graben Square in gloaming deep
Renaissance in spirit climbs once more,
and the Swiss Courtyard so long asleep
I can sense now through the dark Swiss Door.
Softly, early, high baroque caress
sisterly the block's gray ancientness.

More bourgeois a picture now unfolds –
stores are left and right from door to door –
in the late dead Kaiser Leopold's
broadly squatting wing and corridor.
Then through darkened pillars' watchful gloom
I again step into night's black room.

Left the Neue Burg stands strange and far.
Prince Eugene's own frozen shadow stares
blackly upward. In the sky no star.
Does the bronze knight yet await it there?
Unrestrained the winter tempests howl.
From the tower time leers like an owl.

In die Stirne drück' ich meinen Hut.
Knirschend kämpft mein Schritt sich seine Bahn.
Wie ein wilder Stier in blinder Wut
schnaubt ein Auto bösen Blicks heran,
greller Messerstich durch meinen Traum,
dann des äußern Burgtors hoher Raum.

Auf dem Burgring wischt das Lampenlicht
mir mit langen Fingern kalt und klar
letzte Spinnwebfäden vom Gesicht;
taucht ins Wesenlose, was da war.
Eine Straßenbahn bremst scharf und hart.
Ich bin wieder in der Gegenwart.

Firm I press my hat down on my brow.
Grinding on their way my footsteps ply.
Like a wild bull blind with fury now
hither snorts a car with evil eye,
gleaming stab that my dream penetrates,
then high space: the castle's outer gates.

On the Burgring now the lamplight plays,
with its fingers long and cold and clear
wipes last threads of cobweb from my face;
into formlessness dips what was here.
Sharp and hard the braking of a tram –.
In the here and now once more I am.

EMMY KLEIN-SYNEK

WIEN IM FRÜHLING

Einst hörte man in aller Welt
von Wien als Stadt der Lieder sprechen.
Jetzt hat sich noch dazu gesellt
der Name „Stadt der grünen Flächen."

Bezirk kommt nach Bezirk daran.
Nur neidlos noch ein Weilchen warten.
Kaum ziehn sich grün die Bäume an,
blüht überall ein neuer Garten.

Auf Donauufern werden bald
sich junge grüne Flächen breiten,
zur Frühlingslust von Jung und Alt
im goldnen Sonnenglast sich weiten.

Das grüne Wien hat auch gedacht
voll Menschenliebe seiner Blinden,
daß sie in eines Parkes Pracht
lustwandelnd ihre Wege finden.

Die feinen Finger können dann
die Pflanzennamen lesend tasten,
daß jeder sich erwählen kann
den Lieblingsbaum, um dort zu rasten.

Da mag der Himmel frühlingslicht
auf unser Wien herunter blicken,
ihm in das lachende Gesicht
recht viel von seiner Sonne schicken.

VIENNA IN SPRING

Vienna once the town of songs
was called in far-flung places.
With that a new name now belongs:
"The city of the verdant spaces."

In every district it is seen.
Just wait a while, no envy showing.
The trees are hardly decked in green,
bloom everywhere new gardens glowing.

On Danube banks, o'er spaces soon
young greenness outward will be wending,
for young and old a springtime boon
in sun's gold radiance extending.

Vienna green, with love that's real
has not forgotten here its blind,
that they in parks may splendor feel,
may strolling their own pathways find.

Then fingers fine can reading see
the names of plants, the letters testing,
that each can there select a tree,
a favorite for pausing, resting.

Then may the spring-bright sky from space
be down on our Vienna glancing,
and send into his laughing face
rich measure of its sunlight dancing.

MARTINA WIED

SANKT STEPHAN

Für Christine Busta

Dumpf lebt in mir ein Kindertraum:
Die alte Stadt im Flockenflaum,
Rad stockt und Huf, im Schnee verstummt,
Die Menschen eilen pelzvermummt.

Die Kirche groß im Nebel steht,
Ein himmelstrebendes Gebet.
Das warme Licht fällt auf den Stein –
Mich zieht der Weihrauchduft hinein.

Es weint das Wachs am Opferstock,
Die Sünde kniet im schwarzen Rock:
„Was tust du, Seel', mit deinem Pfund?"
Ruft streng ein dunkler Orgelmund.

Das Glöcklein klingt vom Hochaltar,
Des Heilands Leib gleißt wunderbar.
Die Kinderseele schaut und lauscht
Wie Gottes goldener Fittig rauscht.

SAINT STEPHEN'S

For Christine Busta

A child's dream sluggish in me wakes
The city old in downy flakes,
Wheel stops and hoof, grown dumb in snow,
The fur-wrapped people hurry so.

The church in mist stands looming there,
Its striving heavenward, a prayer.
Upon the stone, the warm light falls, –
The scent of incense draws me, calls.

Upon the poor-box hot wax weeps,
In black, sin kneeling vigil keeps:
"What do you, soul, with this your pound?"
Calls sternly dark an organ sound.

From altar high the bell rings fresh,
And wondrous gleams the Saviour's flesh.
The child's pure soul looks and listens,
How God's own golden pinion glistens.

ERIKA MITTERER

STADTPARK

Stille steht die Waage.
Laß uns diese Tage
noch dem Leben traun!
Knospe birst am Strauche
und im linden Hauche
wird die weiße Stirn dir braun.

Überm Teich die Weide
schwankt im Tränenkleide,
lautlos zieht der Schwan.
Krokus sprießt und Primel –
doch im seidnen Himmel
ziehn die großen Totenvögel ihre Bahn.

Liebster, fühl die Tage
dennoch ohne Klage,
alles steht im Saft.
Nichts darf uns verbittern . . .
wollen ohne Zittern
traun des Ungebornen heiler Kraft.

CITY PARK

Still the balance stays.
Let us in these days
trust yet in life's light!
Buds burst forth on trees,
in the gentle breeze
turns to brown your forehead white.

Willow o'er the pond
sways in tear-clothed frond,
soundless moves the swan.
Crocus, primrose bloom –
yet in silk sky's room
move enormous birds of death now on and on.

Dearest, feel the days,
but no mourning raise,
all's in sap and flower.
Naught must us distress . . .
without fearfulness
we will trust the unborn's healthy power.

FRIEDRICH TORBERG

PRATER HAUPTALLEE

Hier ist es immer Sonntag. Luft und Stille
stehn feierlich Spalier. Von ferne trägt
ein Vogelruf sich her, halb eingehegt
in der Kastanienwipfel dichter Fülle.

Wenn braun aus ihrer stachelgrünen Hülle
vom Astwerk eine Frucht zu Boden schlägt,
liegt sie nach kurzem Kollern unbewegt,
als wär's ihr eigner und gemessner Wille.

Und wer sich allzu tief in die Allee
hinein verlor, dem wächst sie in die Weite
und dehnt sich vor- und rückwärts: bis er jäh

stehn bleibt und jäh beklommen Ausschau hält,
und sucht – und weiß nicht mehr, nach welcher Seite –
den Anfang und das Ende und die Welt.

PRATER'S TREE-LINED BOULEVARD

Here it is ever Sunday. Festively
line air and peace the lane. A distant sound
of calling bird floats in, half wrapped around
by chestnut treetops' thick intensity.

When brown from prickly green hull falling free
a fruit leaves branch above and strikes the ground,
it briefly rolls, then lying still is found,
as though it so had willed itself to be.

And who himself into the boulevard
too deeply loses, far from him it grows,
spreads forward, backward, 'til he's brought up hard,

abruptly stops and anxious watches for
and seeks – and to which side no longer knows –
beginning, ending, and the world once more.

BLICK VOM KOBENZL

Daß eine Stadt sich so dem Blick vergönnen,
so groß und nah sein kann! Daß eine Stadt
so satt von Grün ist, so von Häusern matt –
und kannst ein jedes fast beim Namen nennen!

Wenn Kinder sich auf einen Traum besännen –
es wäre dieser Traum und diese Stadt,
die Türme, Kuppeln und ein Flußband hat,
wie sie es nur aus Märchenbüchern kennen.

Nun aber laß vom Stephansturm zum Prater
langsam die Blicke gehn – nein, dorthin schau –
nicht ganz so weit, nur bis zum Burgtheater –

und jetzt nach links – ein Stückchen noch, ein kleines –
wo du das viele Grün siehst – dort, genau:
dort ist mein Haus, Geliebte. Wo ist deines?

VIEW FROM THE KOBENZL

O that a town thus yields itself to view,
can be so great and near! O that a town
its fill of green has, dull with houses grown –
and nearly all are known by name to you!

If children should recall a dream anew,
this dream they would remember and this town,
that towers, domes and band of river crown,
as else alone from storybooks they knew.

But now let from Saint Stephen's to the Prater
your gaze go slowly – no, look over there –
not quite so far, just to the Burgtheater –

now to the left – a little farther yet –
where you see all that green – precisely there:
there is my house. Now where is yours, my pet?

JOSEF WEINHEBER

ALT-OTTAKRING

Was noch lebt, ist Traum.
Ach, wie war es schön!
Jüngre werden kaum
Jene Zeit verstehn,
Wo das Kirchlein stand
Und die Häuser blank
Unterm Giebelrand
Hatten Weingerank.

Und im Herbste gar,
Wenn der Maische Duft
Hing im blauen Klar
Der beschwingten Luft!
Von den Hügeln schlicht
Kam der Hauer Sang,
Da die Stadt noch nicht
Grau ins Grüne drang.

Heut ein Steinbezirk
Wie ein andrer auch,
Und nur sanft Gebirg
Schickt wie einst den Hauch,
Hauch von Obst und Wein
In die Gassen aus,
Und der Sonnenschein
Liegt auf altem Haus.

Da und dort ein Tor
Hat noch breiten Schwung,
Buschen grün davor
Lädt wie einst zum Trunk,
Und im Abend wird
Längst Vergangnes nah,
Spielt ein Bursch gerührt
Ziehharmonika.

OLD OTTAKRING

Dream is living still.
Oh, it was so grand!
Scarcely youth who will
That time understand,
When the chapel small
Stood, and houses bright
"Neath the gables all
Were with vines bedight.

And in autumn too,
When scent May-like fair
Hung in clearness blue
On the quickened air!
Simple from the hill
Vinekeeps' songs came gay,
When the town pressed still
Into green no gray.

Now domain of stone
Like another too,
Gentle hills alone
Send as once anew
Breath of fruit and wine
Out into the lanes,
And the sun's warm shine
On old house remains.

Here and there a door
Still is swinging wide,
Bushes green before,
Bids to drink inside,
And at close of day
Nears what long is gone,
Stirred a fellow plays
His accordion.

LIEBHARTSTAL

Das bißchen Wein, das südwärts noch gedeiht,
lockt manchmal kleine Leute in die Schenken.
Gelächter, Kreischen, Schrammeln, Trunkenheit,
Schaubudenlust, Lampions und Hüteschwenken.

Ein Rest von Wienertum, verfälscht, gestreckt,
so wie der Wein aus den verbliebnen Gärten.
Dienstmädchenelend, festtäglich geschleckt,
Familienzank, Geraunz von Knasterbärten.

Im Herbst jedoch, an einem Wochentag,
ist alles hier wie einst. Kastanien liegen
vom Baum geplatzt am Weg; der Amselschlag
müht sich umsonst, die Stille zu besiegen.

Melancholie streicht sanft durch die Alleen,
liegt als Musik auf den gelösten Lehnen,
Und steigst du höher, siehst du fern und schön
die heißgeliebte Stadt ins Blau sich dehnen.

LIEBHARTSTAL

The wine still grown in gardens to the south
Draws to the inns on Sundays modest people.
Giggling and shrieks, folk quarters, drunkenness,
Hat-waving, Chinese lanterns, puppet shows.

What's left of Viennese essence, watered down
Just like the wine from those remaining plots.
Misery of housemaids dressed in shiny rags,
Family rows, and grouses of old cranks.

Yet in the autumn on a working day
All is as it had been. The chestnuts lie
Along the path cleft open. Blackbirds flute
In vain attempts to overcome the quiet.

Melancholy drifts through the avenues
And flows as music down the soft hillside.
Climb higher. See, stretched far into the blue,
Distant and lovely the beloved town.

ALMA JOHANNA KOENIG

WALDVIERTEL. NIEDERÖSTERREICH

Hügelan und hügelweit,
bis zu Bergen, die uns blau verlocken,
steht – nach später Reise – das Getreid
als des Herbstes Festgezeit in Hocken.
Heidekraut erblüht hier vor dem Schnitt
und der Abend bringt schon Nebel mit.

Blaugeäugt, das Haar schier weiß
spielen Kinder auf gefällten Fichten.
Doch schon pflanzt getreuer Väterfleiß
neue Stämmchen, wo sich Hänge lichten.
Kühl und schmalgesichelt könnt ihr sehen
Herbstmond über ew'gen Wäldern stehen.

WALDVIERTEL. LOWER AUSTRIA

Spreading o'er the hills' domain
to the peaks whose blue enticement weaves, –
after late maturing – stands the grain
as fall's festive tent in heaps of sheaves.
Heather blooms before the harvest here,
mist comes in while night is drawing near.

Blue-eyed, white-haired as can be,
children play on fallen spruce and fir.
But already staunch sires' industry
plants new trees where thinned-out slopes occur.
Fall moon's cool slim crescent you behold
standing over woods eternal, old.

PAULA VON PRERADOVIĆ

OBERÖSTERREICHISCHE LANDSCHAFT

Steiler Turm am Himmelsrand,
Bächlein unter Bäumen,
Hügeliges Apfelland,
Das die Wolken säumen.

Alter Städte Markt und Tor,
Glockenton von ferne,
Überm großen Priel hervor
Erste blasse Sterne.

Landschaft, himmelweit und groß:
Nach der Tage Hasten
Selig war's, in deinem Schoß
Träumerisch zu rasten.

Selig war's, zu dieser Frist
Uns von allem Bösen
In dem Frieden, der du bist,
Linde zu erlösen.

UPPER-AUSTRIAN LANDSCAPE

Tower steep at sky's brink and
Brook beneath trees brimming,
Hilly, rolling apple-land
That the clouds are rimming.

Ancient cities' market, gate,
Distant bell tones surging,
Up above the Priel so great
First pale stars emerging.

Landscape grand and heaven-broad:
After days of bustle
Bliss 'twas dreamily to nod,
In your lap to nestle.

Bliss 'twas in that space of time
From all evil's gleaming
Gently in your peace sublime
Us to be redeeming.

MARTHA HOFFMANN

ALT-AUSSEE

Gründunkler See, von Lärchen, Buchen, Föhren
und steilen Felsenwänden dicht umstellt:
in dich eintauchen, tief dir angehören,
ist Wiederkehr in meine Kinderwelt.

Die Bergesriesen sind nicht kleiner worden,
wie's sonst nach langer Frist erscheinen mag;
noch kenn' ich jeden Steg an deinen Borden
und deiner Plätte eigenen Ruderschlag!

Wenn dann der Loserkamm vom letzten warmen Schimmer,
die Trisselwand im See von Purpur widerstrahlt,
wenn Abendröte selbst das spitze Kirchlein malt –
treten wir leiser in das alte Bauernzimmer;

vom Dachstein grüßt herein unirdisch weißes Leuchten . . .
sind's Regentropfen, die das Aug mir feuchten –?

OLD AUSSEE

Green-darkened lake, surrounded closely, steeply
by rocky walls, by beech and larch and pine:
to dip in you, belong to you so deeply
returns me to that childhood world of mine.

The mountain giants have not lost their size,
as after absence long it may appear;
each path along your shores I recognize,
and your flat skiff's own paddle beat so dear.

When then the Loser Ridge reflects the last warm glowing,
and Trissel Wall from purple lake reflects anew,
when sunset paints the church's pointed steeple too,
into the old farmhouse softly we'll be going;

from Dachstein greets us here a white unearthly shine . . .
do drops of rain now wet these eyes of mine –?

LILLY SAUTER

VOLLMOND IN SALZBURG

Wie kann ich schlafen, wenn im Fenster steht
Die Festung und der Mond,
Wie kann ich schlafen, alle Brunnen rauschen,
Wie kann ich schlafen, wenn der Heuwind weht,
Wie kann ich schlafen in dem langen Lauschen
Auf einen Glockenschlag, der wandern geht.
Wie kann ich schlafen, auf der Brücken bauschen
Sich helle Fahnen und vom Berg gerät
Man an der Kuppeln Dunkelheit. Es lebt
Soviel Musik darin. Es ist nicht spät.
Der Mond ist voll, auf seinem Leuchten schwebt,
Auf Melodien mein Bett,
Wie kann ich schlafen . . .

FULL MOON IN SALZBURG

How can I sleep, when in the window glow
The fortress and the moon,
How can I sleep, the fountains rush and well,
How can I slumber when the hay winds blow,
How can I sleep, long listening for a bell
To send abroad its tones that wand'ring go.
How can I sleep, upon the bridge now swell
The banners bright, and from the hill one's led
Into the darkness of the domes. In there
Lives so much music. 'Tis not late, as yet
The moon is full, floats on its glowing fair,
On melodies my bed,
How can I slumber . . .

NATALIE BEER

MEIN VORARLBERG

O Vorarlberg, ich grüße dich,
mein kleines, treues Heimatland,
wie lieb ich deinen Bodensee
und deiner hohen Firne Schnee,
des jungen Rheines blaues Band,
Mein Vorarlberg, ich grüße dich.

Es schimmern deine Giebel weiß
im Mondlicht, Ländle du!
Den Bretterhag am Wiesensaum
behütet treu ein Apfelbaum.
Sie wissen um der Heimat Ruh,
die all ihr Träume weiß.

Auf schwindelhoher Canisfluh,
da stehen Sterne, Edelweiß.
Ein Alpenrosentraum erblüht
umweht vom Herdenglockenlied.
Land, wenn ich keinen Weg mehr weiß,
dann deck mich deine Erde zu.

MY VORARLBERG

O Vorarlberg, 'tis you I greet,
my little native land so true,
how much I love Lake Constance, Oh!
and your dear lofty mountains' snow,
the youthful Rhine stream's ribbon blue.
My Vorarlberg, 'tis you I greet.

Your gables shimmer white and gleam
in moonlight, little Land!
The wooden fence that bounds the lea
is guarded by an apple tree.
They know the peace of this home land
that knows their each and every dream.

On Canisfluh so high and free
stand stars of edelweiss aglow.
Of alpine rose there blooms a dream
mid herd-bell song on airy stream.
When I a way no longer know,
O land, let your earth cover me.

HERBERT STRUTZ

GNADE DER HEIMAT

(Kärnten)

Ich liebe dich im Glanz der Wolkenzüge,
in jedem Baum, die Rinde rauh gekerbt.
Mir ist, als ob ich deine Äcker trüge
und deine Wälder, herbstlich rot gefärbt.

Ich spüre dich im Harz, im schweren Weine
des Holzes, und im Honig, sommerlang.
Der goldne Mond verzaubert deine Steine
und weckt mich auf zu dunklem Lobgesang.

Auf deinen Bergen weidet meine Seele.
Die Kammer meines Herzens füllt dein Korn.
Und daß ich stets mich wieder dir vermähle,
lockt mich zu dir der Kindheit Fabelhorn.

Ich träume dich selbst noch am fremden Herde,
dir glühend zugetan seit Anbeginn,
und werde Erde sein von deiner Erde,
wenn manche glauben, daß ich nicht mehr bin.

GRACE OF THE HOMELAND

(Carinthia)

I love you in the glow of cloudbanks faring,
in roughly crenate bark of every tree.
I feel as though your farmlands I were bearing
and all your forests, red autumnally.

I feel you in the resin, heavy wine
of wood, and in the honey, summer long.
Your stones are charmed by moon so golden fine
that wakens me to darkly praising song.

Upon your hills my spirit grazes free.
My heart fills all its chambers with your corn.
And that we're wed together constantly,
draws me to you sweet childhood's magic horn.

I dream of you e'en when at foreign hearth,
with fervor from the start attached to you,
and earth then I shall be of your own earth
when many think I've bid this world adieu.

HANS KLOEPFER

SPÄTHERBST IN DER STEIERMARK

Das ist die hohe Zeit in Steier,
wenn hell im Blau die Windmühl schnarrt
und hinterm roten Rebenschleier
die Spindel unterm Preßbaum knarrt.
Ums Haselholz die Meisen jagen,
vom hohen Anger äugt das Reh,
und drüber hin die Almen tragen
heut über Nacht den ersten Schnee.

Des Goldes hat der Tag kein Ende,
das rings auf Frucht und Zweigen glüht,
es werden hundert braune Hände
der Arbeit und der Lust nicht müd.
Dem Auge sind die fernsten Grenzen
ein Wanderfalkenflügelschlag,
wenn sie mit leiser Sehnsucht kränzen
den stillbesonnten Erntetag.

Dann ist's ein warmes Sonnenleuchten,
das spät noch hoch am Berge geht,
wenn nach dem Tal, dem nebelfeuchten,
das Dunkel aus dem Walde späht.
Ein rotes Feuer brennt im Grunde,
Rebhühner rufen sich zur Ruh,
und überm Wald zur Märchenstunde
kommt hoch der Mond im Silberschuh.

Und meines Lebens schwerste Stunden,
all meiner Tage leise Pracht
sie haben sich zur Ruh gefunden
im spiegelklaren See der Nacht.
Mit leisen Schritten kehrt die Seele
durchs müde Land zum Heimathaus
und löscht, daß sie kein Glanz mehr quäle,
still aller Sehnsucht Lichter aus.

LATE AUTUMN IN STYRIA

In Styria, 'tis the glorious time
when bright in blue the windmill squeaks
and back of red grape veil sublime
the spindle 'neath the press-shaft creaks.
Round hazel trees dart titmice fair,
the deer looks out from meadow height,
up further, alpine leas will bear
the season's first soft snow tonight.

No end has this day's golden crown
that round on fruit and branches glows,
not one of hundred hands so brown
of work and pleasure weary grows.
The farthest borders to our view
are but a beat of falcon's wing,
when they with longing soft imbue
the sunlit day of harvesting.

Then 'tis a warm and sunny glow
that late high on the mountain lies
when to the mist-damp vale below
the darkness from the forest spies.
at bottom burns a crimson fire,
the partridge calls to rest now too,
the moon at witching hour comes higher
o'er forest in a silver shoe.

And my life's hours, the heaviest,
all my days' quiet gradeur here,
they now have found their way to rest
within the night's lake mirror-clear.
The soul with soft steps seeks again
through weary land its home tonight,
and, that no glow may bring it pain,
puts out its longing's every light.

MIDA HUBER

HEIMATLIED

(Burgenland)

Dort, wo der See sich in die Weite dehnt,
wo seine rätselhafte Silberflut
vom letzten Saum des Himmels angerührt,
im grünen Schilfwald eingebettet ruht,
ist unsre Heimat. Horch, aus Rohr und Ried,
aus tausend Kehlen tönt ihr süßes Lied!

Und da, wo Furche sich an Furche reiht,
wo Menschenfleiß ums heilge Brot sich müht,
wo Menschenfleiß auf sanftem Hügelland
die Rebe wartet, bis die Traube glüht,
ist unsre Heimat: bis zum letzten Rand
von Sonnenglanz erfüllt das offne Land!

Wo neben Heide, neben reicher Flur
die tiefen, sammetdunklen Wälder weh'n,
geheimnisvoll von Wassern wild durchströmt,
wo noch die alten Mühlenräder gehn,
da sprichst du, Heimat, uns dein liebes Wort:
Daß es so sing', und klinge immerfort!

Wo Dorf und Städtchen freundlich hingestreut,
die mächtge Burg, von Fels und Wald umsäumt,
seit frühen Heldentagen niederschaut,
wo hoch im Turm der kühne Falke träumt,
da zieht Frau Sage ihren Zauberkreis
und singt der schönen Heimat Lob und Preis!

Ja, Heimat, Lob und Preis sei ewig dein!
Du unsres Mühn's und Schaffens bester Sinn!
Gott, der dich hart geprüft, er führe dich
durch eine Zeit des wahren Friedens hin!
Er schlinge eng der Treue goldnes Band
um dich und uns, geliebtes Burgenland!

SONG OF HOME
(Burgenland)

There, where the lake into the distance spreads,
where its mysterious flood with silver sheen,
touched by the heavens' lowest hem,
rests bedded in a bulrush forest green,
our home lies. Hark, from reed and marshy lea,
from myriad throats rings its sweet melody!

And there, where range the furrows row on row,
where industry toils hard for holy bread,
where industry upon the gentle hills
attends the vine until the grape glows red,
our home lies: to the distant verges spanned
with glow of sunlight filled the open land!

Where next to heather, next to fertile field
winds through the deep dark velvet forests blow,
wild enigmatic waters flowing through
where still the ancient wheels of millworks go,
you speak there, home, to us your cherished word:
that it may thus sing on, and e'er be heard!

Where town and village friendly scattered lie,
the mighty castle hemmed by woods and rock
since early hero days has watched above,
where in the tall spire dreams the fearless hawk,
Dame Legend there her magic circle lays
and sings the lovely homeland's glory, praise!

Yes, homeland, glory, praise be ever yours!
Best meaning of our toil and labor, you!
May God who proved you harshly be your guide
on through a time of peace authentic, true!
May He entwine fidelity's gold band
round you and us, belovéd Burgenland!

ERNST WALDINGER

MUSIK FÜR DIESE ZEIT

Was bleibt uns denn im Lichte, das uns blendet,
Im großen Leerlauf, der sich Arbeit nennt,
Wenn sich das Tier, das blind am Göpel rennt,
Des Tempos rühmt, das ihm die Technik spendet,
Eh es erschöpft in ihrem Joche endet.

Uns bleibt, am Abend still die Tür zu schließen,
Wenn der Verkehr sich huppend heiser schrie,
Der Töne kleine Sphärenharmonie,
Die uns die Götter lächelnd überließen,
Im Gleichklang mit dem Herzen zu genießen.

Die Sonne Mozarts, die uns nicht versengt,
Frühsommerwind, der um Akkorde schweift,
Hat im Elysium das Gras gereift,
Im Schauer, der uns süß die Brust beengt,
Hat Wehmut in die Wollust sich gemengt.

Und um den strengen Jubel der Monaden,
Kristallner Kugeln, die im Äther rollen,
Hält Bach in Zügeln eines Wildbachs Grollen,
Und fromm umströmt er sie, mit Sternenschwaden,
Mit Mondenglanz und Sonnenglast beladen.

Und Händel mit der Harfe vor Seraphen,
Die ehern schreitend ihre Harfen schlagen,
Und zwischen Sirius und großem Wagen,
Mit Schäfern flötend neben Wolkenschafen,
Zu goldnem Gloria zusammentrafen.

Und Beethovens Gewitter bricht das Grau;
Versöhnungstränen, die auf Gräsern zittern –
Ein Birkenwald – zu Honigtropfen splittern
Die Strahlen sich an Stämmen – trunkne Schau:
Des stummen Mittags Majestät in Blau.

MUSIC FOR THIS TIME

What's left for us in light that dazzles, friends,
In idle motion that we label moil,
When boasts the blind beast at the winch in toil
Of tempo that technology him lends
Before exhausted in its yoke he ends.

To us remains at eve to close the door
To traffic's honking screams gone hoarse, then we
Enjoy the tones of small sphere-harmony
That smiling gods have left us in sweet store,
In unison with our own hearts once more.

O Mozart's sun, that burns us not with light,
A summer wind that roams around the chords
Has ripened in Elysium the swards,
In thrills that sweetly make our breast feel tight,
In sadness mingled with the pure delight.

Round stern rejoicing of the monads free,
Of crystal balls that through the ether roll,
Holds Bach in reins an angry wild brook's soul,
With swaths of stars and moonglow-laden he
Streams radiant sungleam round them piously.

And Händel with his harp to angels bowed
Who brazen striding strike their harps again
Between great Sirius and Charles's Wain,
With shepherds piping next to sheep of cloud,
Sing gloria together, golden, proud.

And Beethoven's great tempest breaks the gray;
Atonement-tears, that in the grasses shake –
A birch wood – there to drops of honey break
The rays of sun on tree trunks – drunken play:
Mute midday's majesty in blue today.

Wir wollen still die Tür am Abend schließen,
Denn jene kleine Sphärenharmonie,
Die in den Herzen lebt, sie endet nie,
Mag Tag um Tag auch tobender verfließen,
Uns soll der Trott, das Tretwerk nicht verdrießen.

Der Treiber treibt es, wie's ihn selber treibt;
Die Sonne Mozarts, Händels Harfenfrieden,
Beethovens Sturm und Bach, in dem hienieden
Kristallen klingend Gottes Seele leibt . . .
Es is die innere Musik, die bleibt.

Let's softly shut the door at close of day
Because that small sphere-harmony, a friend
That lives on in our hearts will never end,
Though days now ever wilder flow away,
Us shall the trot, the treadwork not dismay.

The driver drives it, as it o'er him reigns;
The sun of Mozart, Händel's harp-peace dear,
Beethoven's storm and Bach, in whom down here
Crystaline ringing, God's soul substance gains . . .
It is the inner music that remains.

EUGENIE FINK

MOZART

Aus Fernen tönt Musik, wir wollen lauschen
Den sanften Tönen, die im Raume rauschen.
Uns grüßen Stimmen aus der Ewigkeit.
Und alle Klänge sind kristall'ne Stufen
Zu den Entrückten, die uns heimlich rufen:
„Nur Übergang ist eure Erdenzeit!"
Und wir verwandeln uns, wir werden Geigen;
Die Gottheit selber will sich lächelnd neigen,
Auf uns zu spielerm, wir sind fromm bereit.
Die sich schon ganz im Irdischen verloren
Sind jäh' begnadet, selig auserkoren
Und tragen nun wie einen Stern ihr Leid.

MOZART

From far the music rings, we'll listen, hear
The gentle tones that in space murmur near.
Here voices greet us from eternity.
And sounding tones are stairs of crystal all
To those beyond who now in secret call:
"A passage mere is your mortality!"
To violins do we transform us now;
Divinity itself will smiling bow
To play us, piously prepared are we.
The ones already lost in earthliness
Are suddenly chosen, blessed with happiness
And bear now like a star their misery.

ERNST WALDINGER

MOZART, KLAVIERKONZERT NR. 20 IN D-MOLL, KV. 466

Wehmut und Anmut sind verschwistert; innig
Rührt hier ein Lächeln an das Leid, das schattend
Den Schmelz des Daseins trübt, so doppelsinnig
Dem Leben gleichend, Lust und Trauer gattend,
Dem Tode ernst sein Jagdgebiet gestattend.

O edle Klage, ohne anzuklagen,
O Melodie, die Tränen nicht verhehlend,
Die so sich selber, ohne zu verzagen,
Zu Ende singt, o leises Feuer schwelend,
Die Wonne und das Weh der Welt beseelend!

O sanfter Rausch der Schwermut, o wie beut
Musik zum Tanz die Hand hier, wie des Schwebens
Melancholie sich hier ermißt, erfreut!
Gedämpft klingt der Triumphgesang des Lebens:
Vergänglich leben wir, doch nicht vergebens.

„AUCH IST DAS KLOPFENDE HERZ SCHON ANGEZEIGT"

(Mozart Brief über die Arie „O wie ängstlich"
aus der „Entführung aus dem Serail", 28. X. 1781)

Ach, immer klopft in deinen Melodien
Das Menschenherz, und uns wird warm zumut;
Die Lerche jubelt: Siehe, sie ist gut,
Die Welt, die uns der Schöpfungstag verliehn.

„Dem Liebenden wird alle Schuld verziehn",
Klingt deine Botschaft, selbst die dunkle Glut,
Der Sonnenuntergänge Wehmut, ruht
In dem Andante deiner Symphonien

MOZART, PIANO CONCERTO NO. 20 IN D MINOR, K.466

Sadness and grace are closely linked, with feeling
A smile here touches at the pain that shading,
Clouds being's glaze; clear meaning not revealing
Resembling life, delight and sorrow mating,
Death gravely on its hunt-ground tolerating.

O noble grievance, without accusation,
O melody, unhidden teardrops showing,
That thus itself, without despaired cessation,
Sings to its end, o soft fire slowly glowing,
The world's delight and woe with life endowing.

O sadness' gentle rapture, o how here
The music bids to dance, how floating free
Here sadness grasps itself and brings good cheer!
Subdued resounds life's song of victory:
We live as transients, but not uselessly.

"EVEN THE BEATING HEART IS ALREADY INDICATED"

(Mozart letter about the aria "O How Fearful" from the *Abduction from the Seraglio*, 10/28/1781)

Oh, ever beats within your melodies
The heart of man, and warm in mood we grow
The lark exults: See, good's the world below,
Us given by creation day's decrees.

"Forgiv'n all lover's liabilities,"
Rings out your message, e'en the darkling glow,
The sunset's melancholy, resting so
In the andante of your symphonies.

Wie Abendrot in einem Alpensee,
Daß keiner weiß, ob wonnig ihm, ob weh
Die Brust erschauert; eine Träne schwingt

Ihm auf der Wimper, doch dein Lächeln singt
Schon weiter, Trost und Tau für seine Seele . . .
Heut sucht Musik, wie sie uns schärfer quäle.

BEETHOVENSONATE

Lust und Trauer halten sich umschlungen,
Und ihr Keuchen wird zum Harfenton,
Lassen sich und stehn, die wild gerungen,
Von der eigen Musik bezwungen,
Lauschen sie beschämt und schreiten stumm davon.

Und in Eichen fährt ein Sturmeswille,
Wühlt im Korn und jauchzt und zaust den Mohn —
Lauter singt und atemlos die Grille
Und den Raum der andachtsvollen Stille
Füllt die Stimme Gottes orgelschwellend schon.

Sieh, du bist schon über allen Nöten,
Und dein Klang befreit sich aus der Fron!
Und dem Lied der schäferlichen Flöten
Folgt ein Flammenchor von Abendröten
Und der Eisenschritt der himmlischen Legion.

Like alpine lake red from the sunset's kiss
That none knows whether it is pain or bliss
That thrills the breast; and there a teardrop swings

Upon his eyelash, yet your smile there sings
Already on, for his soul comfort, dew . . .
Now music would that our pain sharper grew.

BEETHOVEN SONATA

Pleasure, sadness hold each other caught,
And their gasps a lovely harp tone play,
Loose themselves and stand, who wildly fought,
By their own sweet music brought to naught,
Listen they ashamed, stride silently away.

Into oak trees moves a tempest's will,
Stirs the grain, shouts, tugs the poppies gay,
Louder sings the cricket, breathless, shrill,
And the space that is devoutly still
God's voice fills with swelling organ sounds today.

See, already you transcend all need,
And your tone springs free from labor's fray,
And the songs of shepherd flutes indeed
Now a flaming choir of sunsets lead
And the iron tread of heaven's vast array.

MICHAEL KLIEBA

SCHUBERT

Ein Echo läuft durch den Wiener Wald
Im Wiesengrund, auf der Bergeshald,
Und wo ein Vogel lustig singt,
Ein Bächlein über Kiesel springt
Und flappernd sich ein Mühlrad dreht
Und vor dem Haus ein Mägdlein steht –
In blauer Luft und Sonnenschein –
Da läuft das Echo hintendrein.

Ein Wandersmann geht durch den Wald,
Der hört das ferne Echo bald
Und läuft ihm nach mit frohem Sinn:
Da steht die schöne Müllerin –
Wie er das holde Mädchen sieht,
Erblüht im Herzen ihm ein Lied –
In blauer Luft und Sonnenschein
Fängt er des Waldes Echo ein.

Und immer schneller wird sein Schritt,
Er nimmt das liebe Echo mit
Mit Blumen, Bach und Vogelsang
Und mit dem lauten Mühlradgang,
Trägt's in die Stadt, daß alles glaubt,
Der Wald rauscht jedem um das Haupt . . .
Wer's Echo fing? Nun rat' einmal!
Schulmeister war er in Lichtental.

SCHUBERT

Through Vienna's woods an echo glides,
In grassy hollow, on mountainsides,
And where a songbird gaily sings,
A brooklet over pebbles springs
And clanking turns a millwheel, and
Before the house a maiden stands –
In azure air and sunlight's glow –
There runs the echo to and fro.

A hiker walks the woodland dear,
The echo far he soon can hear
With joy he follows it: And there:
Now stands the miller's daughter fair –
As he the lovely maid espies
Within his heart a song does rise –
In sunlight's glow and azure air
He captures the woods' echo there.

And ever faster move his feet
He takes along the echo sweet
With flowers, brook and song of bird,
The millwheel's clatter that he's heard,
Takes it to town, that all suppose
the sough of woods round each head blows . . .
Now guess who's caught the echo's call!
A schoolmaster in Lichtental.

FRIEDRICH HALM

MEIN HERZ, ICH WILL DICH FRAGEN

Mein Herz, ich will dich fragen,
Was ist denn Liebe, sag'? –
„Zwei Seelen und ein Gedanke,
Zwei Herzen und ein Schlag!"

Und sprich, woher kommt Liebe? –
„Sie kommt und sie ist da!"
Und sprich, wie schwindet Liebe? –
„Die war's nicht, der's geschah!"

Und was ist reine Liebe? –
„Die ihrer selbst vergißt!"
Und wann ist Lieb' am tiefsten? –
„Wenn sie am stillsten ist!"

Und wann ist Lieb' am reichsten? –
„Das ist sie, wenn sie gibt!"
Und sprich, wie redet Liebe? –
„Sie redet nicht, sie liebt!"

MY HEART, I WANT TO ASK YOU

My heart, I want to ask you,
What is then love, so sweet? –
"Two spirits and one idea,
Two hearts and but one beat!"

And tell me, whence does love come? –
"It comes and it is there!"
And say, how does love dwindle? –
"'Twas none, that so did fare!"

And pure love, what is that then? –
"'Tis selfless love, the best!"
And when is love the deepest? –
"When it is quietest!"

And when is love the richest? –
"'Tis when to give it seeks!"
And say, how does love talk then? –
"It loves, it never speaks!"

NIKOLAUS LENAU

AN DIE ENTFERNTE

Diese Rose pflück ich hier,
In der fremden Ferne;
Liebes Mädchen, dir, ach dir
Brächt ich sie so gerne!

Doch bis ich zu dir mag ziehn
Viele weite Meilen,
Ist die Rose längst dahin,
Denn die Rosen eilen.

Nie soll weiter sich ins Land
Lieb von Liebe wagen,
Als sich blühend in der Hand
Läßt die Rose tragen;

Oder als die Nachtigall
Halme bringt zum Neste,
Oder als ihr süßer Schall
Wandert mit dem Weste.

TO HER FAR AWAY

Here in foreign land this rose
I have gathered sadly
And would take this rose I chose
To you, dear girl, gladly.

But ere back to you I fly
Over hill and valley,
Wither will the rose and die;
Roses cannot dally.

Let not ever farther stray
Love from love and lover
Than a rose in bloom will stay,
In a cupped hand's cover,

Than a nesting nightingale
Roams for twigs and grasses,
Than its song down through the vale
With the west wind passes.

KARL KRAUS

VERWANDLUNG

Stimme im Herbst, verzichtend über dem Grab
auf deine Welt, du blasse Schwester des Monds,
süße Verlobte des klagenden Windes,
schwebend unter fliehenden Sternen –

raffte der Ruf des Geists dich empor zu dir selbst?
nahm ein Wüstensturm dich in dein Leben zurück?
Siehe, so führt ein erstes Menschenpaar
wieder ein Gott auf die heilige Insel!

Heute ist Frühling. Zitternder Bote des Glücks,
kam durch den Winter der Welt der goldene Falter.
Oh knieet, segnet, hört, wie die Erde schweigt.
Sie allein weiß um Opfer und Thräne.

AUFERSTEHUNG

Mein Haupt war Flamme, dem beschwingten Schritt
entstiebten Funken, als ich von dir eilte.
Ich riß mir die Minute mit,
wo uns die Ewigkeit verweilte!

So ist das alte Wunder wieder wahr.
Es half ein Gott die Endlichkeit besiegen.
So ist ein müdes Menschenpaar
zu jungen Tagen aufgestiegen!

Mit beiden Händen trag' ich zitternd mir
dein Herz, das die Vergänglichkeit umfangen.
So werde ich zu dir gelangen!
So bin ich auf dem Weg zu mir!

TRANSFORMATION

Voice in the fall renouncing your world
above the grave, you sister, pale, of the moon,
sweet fianceé of the wind that is wailing,
floating under the stars that are fleeing –

snatched you the spirit's call then aloft to your self?
Did a desert storm take you back into your life?
See, thus a new first human pair
led by a god again to the island so holy!

Spring's here today. A quivering herald of bliss
came through the winter of earth the butterfly golden.
Oh kneel and bless and hear how the earth is still.
Earth alone knows of sacrifice, weeping.

RESURRECTION

My head was flame, from steps elated, free,
sprayed sparks, as from you me they quickly carried.
The minute then I took with me,
where time unending for us tarried.

Thus is the ancient wonder true again.
A god assisted finiteness to slay.
So has a weary couple then
ascended to a youthful day!

With trembling hands I carry unto me
your heart, that transitoriness encloses.
So shall I reach you ere life closes!
So am I on the way to me!

HANS LEIFHELM

MIT DEM SICHELMOND, MIT DEM ABENDSTERN

Auch im fremden Land,
Wo ich dir so fern,
Wo ich lange schon verschollen war,
Strahlt dein Angesicht
Mit dem Abendstern,
Weht am nächtigen Himmel hin dein Haar,
Tanzt dein schlanker Fuß
Mit dem Sichelmond,
Winkt mir lieblich deine weiße Hand,
Grüßt dein Lächeln mich,
Das im Lichte wohnt,
Süßer Trost im bittern Menschenland.

Durch die Fluren geht
Kühl der Abendwind,
Silbersaiten klingen deinem Tanz.
Dunkle Brandung ruht,
Und das Leid verrinnt,
Silberwolken spiegeln deinen Glanz.
Eine Stimme süß
Ist im Tal erwacht,
Horch ein Nachtigallenflöten fern,
In Vergessenheit
Hüllt mich ein die Nacht
Mit dem Sichelmond und Abendstern.

WITH THE CRESCENT MOON, WITH THE EVENING STAR

In the foreign land,
Where I was so far
From you, where I long was missing, there
Shines your countenance
With the evening star,
Blows against the night-dark sky your hair,
Dance your slender feet
With the crescent moon,
Lovely beckons me your small white hand,
Greets me too your smile
From the light, a boon,
Comfort sweet in bitter human land.

Through cool meadows walks
Wind at end of day,
Silver strings accompany your dance,
Dark surf lies at rest,
And woe dies away,
Silver clouds reflect your countenance.
And a voice so sweet
Wakens in the vale,
Hear a singing nightingale afar,
In oblivion
Wraps me night's soft veil
With the crescent moon and evening star.

Über fremder Welt
Winkt dein holder Gruß,
Winkt dein Lächeln, deine weiße Hand,
Mit dem Sichelmond
Schreitet schlank dein Fuß,
Kühler Tau rinnt nieder auf das Land.
Fern am Himmel hin
Weht dein nächtiges Haar,
Wendet nieder sich dein Angesicht,
Mit dem Abendstern
Strahlt dein Haupt so klar,
Meines dunklen Lebens schönes Licht.

O'er the foreign world
Waves your greeting fair,
Waves your smile and your white dainty hand,
With the crescent moon
Strides your slim foot there,
Cooling dew runs down upon the land.
In the far sky blows
Your hair dark and dear,
And your face turns downward here to me,
With the evening star
Shines your head so clear,
Gives my dark life light that's fair to see.

ALEXANDER LERNET-HOLENIA

ASOKAS LIEBESLIED

Ach, daß ich deine Wangen
an den meinen, dein Haar
spürte! Wie lang vergangen
ist, was gestern war,
oder eine Sage,
daß ich bei dir lag!
Waren es tausend Tage,
war es nur ein Tag?

Daß ich im Dunkel das Blonde
deiner Locken nicht sah,
nur deine Augen wie Monde,
– dein Atem wie Rosen nah, –
ach, die Sternenprächte
über uns entfacht,
waren es tausend Nächte,
war es nur eine Nacht?

Wog' um Woge spülte
Rosenperlen her
und der Meerwind wühlte
in einem Rosenmeer!
Liebe hielt in Waage
Mond und Sonnenpracht,
einen Tag, tausend Tage,
tausend und eine Nacht!

ASOKA'S LOVE SONG

Oh, that I felt the touch of
your cheeks on mine, your hair!
How long is gone so much of
what yesterday was there,
or a tale, illusion,
that I by you lay!
Were there days in profusion,
was it just one day?

That I in darkness your flowing
curls of blond did not see,
only your eyes like moons glowing,
– like roses your breath near me, –
oh, the starry sights then
that above us shone,
were there a thousand nights then,
was it one night alone?

Rolling waves were washing
pearls of rose to me,
ocean wind was splashing
in a rosy sea!
Love in balance holding
Moon and sunlit sights.
one day, a thousand unfolding
one and a thousand nights.

LILLY SAUTER

SEHNSUCHT

Ich möchte bei dir sein,
wenn der Regen fällt
und unser Bett
eine Insel wird
in seinem Rauschen.

Ich möchte bei dir sein,
wenn der Wind weht
und deine Arme
der Hafen sind
für die Segel der Sehnsucht.

Ich möchte bei dir sein,
wenn die Sonne scheint
und der Mond
und die Sterne sich spiegeln
in deinen Augen.

Denn ich höre den Regen
und fühle den Wind
auch ohne dich,
aber die Lichter des Himmels
vergessen ihr Leuchten,
wenn ich allein bin.

CHRISTINE BUSTA

JAHRESZEITEN

Und Nacht für Nacht fiel Schnee vor meinem Fenster,
Er fiel so leise wie verschwiegne Trauer.
Am Morgen war mein Garten ganz verschneit.

Ich weiß nicht, wo du schliefst. Gewiß war Frühling
In fremden Gärten. Alle wollen blühen.
Die Liebe lebt vom Wunder, nicht vom Recht.

Für jede Stunde, die du fern warst, hob ich
Dir eine Flocke auf. Ich find sie nimmer.
Nun wird es wohl vor fremden Fenstern schnei'n.

LILLY SAUTER

LONGING

I'd like to be with you
when the raindrops fall
and our own bed
then becomes an isle
amid rain's rushing.

I'd like to be with you
when the wind blows
and your arms
are the harbor
for the sails of longing.

I'd like to be with you
when the sun shines
and the moon
and the stars are reflected
within your eyes.

For I hear the raindrops
and I feel the wind
without you too,
but the lights of the heavens
forget their own glowing
when I am alone.

SEASONS

And night for night snow fell before my window,
It fell as softly as secluded sadness.
And mornings was my garden decked with snow.

I know not where you slept. 'Twas surely springtime
In foreign gardens. All desire to blossom.
And love lives from the wonder, not from right.

For every hour you were far away I
Preserved a flake for you. I'll find them never.
No doubt snow falls before strange windows now.

HERBERT STRUTZ

MÄDCHEN IM FRÜHLING

Im Frühling, wenn die Gärten neu erwachen,
gehn alle Mädchen wie in einem Traum.
Von ihren Mienen pflückt der Wind das Lachen
und hängt es wie papierne, bunte Drachen
sanft flatternd in den hellsten Blütenbaum.

Sie wachen auf aus ihrem großen Schweigen
und wissen nicht, was sie dazu befiehlt:
die Abende? die Sterne in den Zweigen–?
Ganz plötzlich fühlen sie sich so wie Geigen,
die sich nach Einem sehnen, der sie spielt.

Da glänzt ein Lächeln, wie dem Tau entnommen,
auf ihren Mienen, die vorübergehn.
Denn ihre Herzen ahnen schon beklommen:
es wird ein sanftes, süßes Wunder kommen.
Nur wissen sie es noch nicht recht: durch wen.

MAIDENS IN SPRING

In springtime, when the gardens new are waking,
The maidens wander all as though in dream.
And from their faces wind is laughter taking
And hangs it soft like kites of paper shaking
Up in the brightest blossom-tree agleam.

They waken from their silence grand, not knowing
Just what commands them waken from their daze.
The evenings? the stars in branches glowing –?
Quite suddenly, they've feelings overflowing
Like violins that long for one who plays.

Then glows a smile as from the dew of morning,
Upon their faces that are passing by.
Because their hearts uneasy catch the warning:
A sweet soft wonder there will come a-borning.
Who brings it, they still can't identify.

OTTO STOESSL

LIEBE

Als ein Jüngling liebt' ich die Geliebte,
Wie der Schiffer seinem guten Stern folgt.
Heute treib' ich hin mit losem Steuer
Unter tausend hohen Lichtern.
Alternd lieb' ich alle, alle lieb' ich,
Liebe lieb' ich, bin den Sternen offen
Allen wie der dunkle Grund des Himmels.

LOVE

As a young man I loved my beloved
As his lucky star a seaman follows.
But today I drive with unmanned rudder
'Neath a thousand lofty lanterns.
Aging, love I all, and all I love now,
Love I love, am to the stars wide open
To them all like heaven's dark foundation.

HUGO ZUCKERMANN

REITERLIED

Drüben am Wiesenrand
Hocken zwei Dohlen –
Fall' ich am Donaustrand?
Sterb' ich in Polen?
Was liegt daran?!
Eh' sie meine Seele holen,
Kämpf' ich als Reitersmann.

Drüben am Ackerrain
Schreien zwei Raben –
Werd' ich der erste sein,
Den sie begraben?
Was ist dabei?!
Viel Hunderttausend traben
In Öst'reichs Reiterei.

Drüben im Abendrot
Fliegen zwei Krähen
Wann kommt der Schnitter Tod,
Um uns zu mähen?
Es ist nicht schad'!
Seh' ich nur unsere Fahnen wehen
Auf Belgerad!

CAVALRY SONG

At yonder meadow's rand
Crouch jackdaws twain –
Fall I on Danube's strand?
'S Poland my bane?
What do I care
Ere they can my soul obtain
I'll fight, a trooper there.

From yonder balk ridge there
Two ravens cry –
Will they to grave me bear
Am I the first to die?
What's it to me?
Hundreds of thousands ride,
In Austria's cavalry.

In yonder sunset sky
Fly there two crows –
When comes death the reaper by
Us for to mow?
It's nothing sad
If I but see our banners blow
O'er Belgerad.

JOSEF LUITPOLD

TROTZIGER ABSCHIED

Wenn das Eisen mich mäht,
wenn mein Atem vergeht,
sollt stumm unterm Rasen mich breiten!
Laßt das Wortegespiel.
's war kein Held, der da fiel.
's war ein Opfer verlorener Zeiten.

's war einer, der nie
nach Völkerblut schrie.
's war ein Bürger erst kommender Zeiten.
Wenn das Eisen mich mäht,
wenn mein Atem vergeht,
sollt stumm unterm Rasen mich breiten!

DEFIANT FAREWELL

When the iron me mows,
when my breath from me goes,
then still neath the greensward me lay!
Leave the word-play as well.
'Twas no hero who fell.
'Twas a sacrifice of a lost day.

'Twas one who ne'er could
demand nations' blood.
'Twas a burgher of some future day.
When the iron me mows,
when my breath from me goes,
then still neath the greensward me lay!

KARL KRAUS

DER STERBENDE SOLDAT

Hauptmann, hol her das Standgericht!
Ich sterb' für keinen Kaiser nicht!
Hauptmann, du bist des Kaisers Wicht!
Bin tot ich, salutier' ich nicht!

Wenn ich bei meinem Herrn wohn',
ist unter mir des Kaisers Thron,
und hab' für sein Geheiß nur Hohn!
Wo ist mein Dorf? Dort spielt mein Sohn.

Wenn ich in meinem Herrn entschlief,
kommt an mein letzter Feldpostbrief.
Es rief, es rief, es rief, es rief!
Oh, wie ist meine Liebe tief!

Hauptmann, du bist nicht bei Verstand,
daß du mich hast hieher gesandt.
Im Feuer ist mein Herz verbrannt
Ich sterbe für kein Vaterland!

Ihr zwingt mich nicht, ihr zwingt mich nicht!
Seht, wie der Tod die Fessel bricht!
So stellt den Tod vors Standgericht!
Ich sterb', doch für den Kaiser nicht!

VOLKSHYMNE

Gott erhalte, Gott beschütze
vor dem Kaiser unser Land!
Mächtig ohne seine Stütze,
sicher ohne seine Hand!
Ungeschirmt von seiner Krone,
stehn wir gegen diesen Feind:
Nimmer sei mit Habsburgs Throne
Österreichs Geschick vereint!

THE DYING SOLDIER

Captain, the drumhead court bring nigh!
I'll not for any Kaiser die!
Captain, you are the Kaiser's guy!
I'll not salute when dead am I!

When I then my Lord God shall see,
I'll have the Kaiser's throne 'neath me,
and for his will but mockery!
My town, my son, where can they be?

When I in my Lord God have died,
will my last letter homeward ride.
It cried, it cried, it cried, it cried!
How deep my love is and how wide!

Captain, you surely are insane,
to send me here and nothing gain.
My heart's burned up in fiery pain.
For no homeland I meet my bane.

You can't force me, you can't force me!
Death breaks the shackles now, o see!
So now let death court-martialed be!
I die, not for His Majesty!

NATIONAL FOLK HYMN

May God save, protect we pray
from the Kaiser, this our land!
Mighty we without his stay,
and secure without his hand!
Unprotected by his crown
we'll face any enemy:
Ne'er be joined to Habsburg's throne
Austria's great destiny!

Fromm und bieder? Wahr und offen
laßt für Recht und Pflicht uns stehn!
Nimmermehr, so laßt uns hoffen,
werden in den Kampf wir gehn!
Eingeheizt die Lorbeerreiser,
die das Heer so oft sich wand!
Gut und Blut für keinen Kaiser!
Friede für das Vaterland!

Was des Bürgers Fleiß geschaffen,
schützet keines Kriegers Kraft!
Nicht dem Geist verfluchter Waffen
diene Kunst und Wissenschaft!
Segen sei dem Land beschieden;
Ruhm und Wahn, sie gelten gleich:
Gottes Sonne strahl' in Frieden
auf ein glücklich Österreich!

Laßt uns fest zusammenhalten,
in der Eintracht liegt die Macht!
Mit vereinter Kräfte Walten
wird das Schwerste leicht vollbracht.
Laßt uns, eins durch Brüderbande,
gleichem Ziel entgegengehn:
Ohne Kaiser glückts dem Lande –
dann wird Österreich ewig stehn!

Uns gehört, was Gott verwaltet,
uns im allerhöchsten Sinn,
reich an Reiz, der nie veraltet –
Reich der Huld, arm an Gewinn!
Was an Glück zuhöchst gepriesen,
gab Natur mit holder Hand.
Heil den Wäldern, Heil den Wiesen,
Segen diesem schönen Land!

Pious, worthy? True, sincere,
let us stand for duty and right!
Never, let us hope now here,
we'll go into any fight!
Let's set fire to army's laurels
which for itself so oft it wound!
For no Kaiser, goods and blood!
Peace be to the Fatherland!

What the townsman's work created
guard no soldier's strength and heart!
Let cursed weaponry be aided
by no science, by no art!
Blest let be our patria
like rate madness and renown.
On a happy Austria
Let in peace the Lord's sun shine!

Let us fast united be,
for in concord lies the might!
With the strength of unity
is the hardest task made light.
Let's, one through fraternal bands
toward our goal together fly:
Kaiser gone: bloom will the land
then Austria will never die!

What God rules is ours to hold,
ours in the highest sense,
rich in charm that ne'er grows old –
Grace-realm, poor in recompense!
Luck's most praised felicities
nature gave with gracious hand.
Hail the forests, hail the leas!
Blessings to this lovely land!

SILVESTER 1917

Dies alte Jahr versank so wehrlos
und aus der Mördergrube steht ein neues auf.
Sind denn die lieben Zeiten ehrlos?
Hemmt keine Scham der Jahre Lauf?

Ein frommes Ohr horcht in die Weiten:
nur manchmal bebt es in der Erde Raum.
Doch unerschüttert gehn die Zeiten
vorüber diesem Sündentraum.

Sie laufen fort mit den Kalendern,
im neuen Jahr das alte Werk zu fördern.
Und nehmen Abschied von der Menschheit Mördern
und sagen Prosit zu der Schöpfung Schändern.

FLIEDER

Nun weiß ich doch, 's ist Frühling wieder.
Ich sah es nicht vor so viel Nacht
und lange hatt' ich's nicht gedacht.
Nun merk' ich erst, schon blüht der Flieder.

Wie fand ich das Geheimnis wieder?
Man hatte mich darum gebracht.
Was hat die Welt aus uns gemacht!
Ich dreh' mich um, da blüht der Flieder.

Und danke Gott, er schuf mich wieder,
indem er wieder schuf die Pracht.
Sie anzuschauen aufgewacht,
so bleib' ich stehn. Noch blüht der Flieder.

NEW YEAR'S EVE 1917

This old year sank so weak, defenseless
and from the cutthroats' den a new one now appears.
Are these times without honor, shameless?
Does no shame slow the passing years?

A pious ear harks in the distance:
from time to time it trembles in earth's space.
Unmoved, the time of our existence
draws past this sin-filled dream apace.

To give the old work stimulation
this coming year, with calendars they're running.
They bid farewell to mankind's killers cunning
and drink a toast to those who rape creation.

LILACS

I know it now, once more 'tis spring.
For so much night, I did not see,
it long has not occurred to me:
I see now lilacs blossoming.

How did I find that wondrous thing
Anew? they'd taken it from me.
O what the world has made us be!
I turn, still lilacs blossoming.

Thank God, He me new life did bring
by bringing new this pomp to be.
I stop awake it now to see.
The lilacs still are blossoming.

ZUM EWIGEN FRIEDEN

> „Bei dem traurigen Anblick nicht sowohl der Übel, die das menschliche Geschlecht aus Naturursachen drücken, als vielmehr derjenigen, welche die Menschen sich untereinander selbst anthun, erheitert sich doch das Gemüth durch die Aussicht, es könne künftig besser werden; und zwar mit uneigennützigem Wohlwollen, wenn wir längst im Grabe sein und die Früchte, die wir zum Teil selbst gesät haben, nicht einernten werden."

Nie las ein Blick, von Thränen übermannt,
ein Wort wie dieses von Immanuel Kant.

Bei Gott, kein Trost des Himmels übertrifft
die heilige Hoffnung dieser Grabesschrift.

Dies Grab ist ein erhabener Verzicht:
„Mir wird es finster, und es werde Licht!"

Für alles Werden, das am Menschsein krankt,
stirbt der Unsterbliche. Er glaubt und dankt.

Ihm hellt den Abschied von dem dunklen Tag,
daß dir noch einst die Sonne scheinen mag.

Durchs Höllentor des Heute und Hienieden
vertrauend träumt er hin zum ewigen Frieden.

Er sagt es, und die Welt ist wieder wahr,
und Gottes Herz erschließt sich mit „und zwar"

Urkundlich wird es; nimmt der Glaube Teil,
so widerfährt euch das verheißne Heil.

O rettet aus dem Unheil euch zum Geist,
der euch aus euch die guten Wege weist!

TOWARD ETERNAL PEACE

> "At the unhappy sight of not only the miseries that oppress the human race from natural causes, but more especially those which men bring upon each other, the spirit is nonetheless gladdened by the prospect that it could become better in the future; namely through unselfish benevolence, when we are long in the grave and unable to harvest the fruits that we ourselves in part have sown."

Ne'er tear-filled glance read as significant
a thought as this one by Immanuel Kant.

By God, exceed no heaven's comfortings
the sacred hope that here this epitaph brings.

This grave is a sublime renunciation:
"The darkness comes, o send illumination!"

For all growth that from being man is ill,
th' immortal dies. Believe and thank he will.

From him it brightens parting from dark day
that someday you will see the sunshine's play.

Below here and through hell's gate of today
in faith to eternal peace he dreams his way.

He says it and the world again is true,
with "namely" God's heart opens up to you.

Authentic it becomes; if faith takes part
the promised grace to you it will impart.

Escape from harm, flee to the spirit who
out of yourselves points out good ways for you!

Welch eine Menschheit! Welch ein hehrer Hirt!
Weh dem, den der Entsager nicht beirrt!

Weh, wenn im deutschen Wahn die Welt verschlief
das letzte deutsche Wunder, das sie rief!

Bis an die Sterne reichte einst ein Zwerg.
Sein irdisch Reich war nur ein Königsberg.

Doch über jedes Königs Burg und Wahn
schritt eines Weltalls treuer Untertan.

Sein Wort gebietet über Schwert und Macht
und seine Bürgschaft löst aus Schuld und Nacht.

Und seines Herzens heiliger Morgenröte
Blutschande weicht: daß Mensch den Menschen töte.

Im Weltbrand bleibt das Wort ihr eingebrannt:
Zum ewigen Frieden von Immanuel Kant!

How evil's man! This prince, how noble, staid!
Woe him whom the renouncer won't dissuade!

Woe, if deluded now the world slept through
the final German wonder called to view!

To reach up to the stars a dwarf's gaze deigned.
A Königsberg his earthly realm remained.

Yet o'er each king's delusion, walled abode
a universe's faithful subject strode.

His words are ruling over sword and might,
and his assurance frees from guilt and night.

To his heart's holy dawn blood guilt will yield:
that man the sword against his brother wield.

Now burned into a world in holocaust,
Kant's "to eternal peace" must ne'er be lost.

FRANZ THEODOR CSOKOR

HEIMKEHR 1918

Unsere Mütter sind gestorben
Unsere Frauen sind alt.
Unsere Häuser sind verdorben,
Überall war Gewalt . . .

Wo sollen wir sitzen und speisen?
Was ist unser Vaterland?
Ein Boden aus Blut und Eisen
Und ein Himmel voll Brand.

Wenn wir unsern Kindern begegnen,
Sie werden uns nicht mehr verstehn.
Wir wollen sie schweigend segnen
Und weiter gehn . . .

THE RETURN HOME 1918

Dead are our mothers, whom we cherished,
Bent are our wives now with age.
Spoiled are our houses, many perished,
Everywhere force did rage . . .

Where should we now sit, eat our food?
And what is our fatherland?
A land made of iron and blood
And skies that blazing stand.

When we meet our children, no more
Will they understand us today.
We'll silently bless them before
We go our way . . .

BERTHOLD VIERTEL

DER FEBRUAR

Da ich in der Welt zerstreut war,
Hörte ich aus Wien die Kunde,
Wie sie ging von Mund zu Munde,
Unbegreiflich, unbestreitbar:

Was im Februar geschehen,
Wie ihr Ordnung dort geschaffen,
Als ihr wagtet, eure Waffen
Gegen euer Volk zu drehen.

Diese frevelnden Kanonen,
Konnte sie die Kirche segnen?
Ließ der Herrgott Eisen regnen,
Wo des Volkes Kinder wohnen?

Habt ihr so den Streit geschlichtet,
So gelöst die Schwierigkeiten?
Wie in frühsten Kaiserzeiten
Waren Galgen aufgerichtet.

Hofftet so ihr zu verjagen
Räuber, Mörder von den Grenzen?
Generale, Eminenzen,
Dieses werdet ihr beklagen!

Bitter werdet bald ihr büßen
Den Verrat an Volkes Söhnen.
Kirchenglocken werden dröhnen,
Den Eroberer zu begrüßen.

Rechenschaft wird er verlangen,
Der das böse Beispiel säte.
Eh' der Hahn noch dreimal krähte,
Ist die Ernte aufgegangen.

FEBRUARY

As I life abroad endured,
From Vienna news I heard,
As went mouth to mouth the word,
Inconceivable, assured:

What took place in February,
How you there new order wrought,
As you with your weapons fought,
Dared them 'gainst your folk to carry.

Those blaspheming guns of hell,
Could they consecration gain?
Did God let the iron rain,
Where the nation's children dwell?

Have you strife's end thus effected
Thus solved problems, ended crimes?
As in earliest Kaiser-times,
Were the gallows there erected.

Hoped you thus to drive away
Killers, thieves from border fences?
Generals and Eminences,
This you will bewail one day!

Bitterly you soon will pay
For betraying your own people.
Bells will sound from church and steeple,
Greet the conqueror on his way.

He'll account of him demand
Who bad precedent did sow.
Ere the cock yet thrice could crow,
Up the crop comes on the land.

Seht, wie eure anmutreichen
Töchter ihm, der einzieht, huldigen!
Und es fallen, mit den Schuldigen,
Menschenopfer ohnegleichen.

Diese schmachgebeugte Erde
Zeugte selbst sich den Diktator.
Und es treibt der Usurpator
Oesterreich zur deutschen Herde.

AUSWANDERER

Nun müssen wir von allem scheiden,
Was Kindheit uns und Wachstum war.
Wir sollen selbst die Sprache meiden,
Die unserer Herzen Wort gebar.

Die Landschaft werden wir verlassen,
Die uns auf ihren Armen trug.
Wir sollen diese Wälder hassen
Und hatten ihrer nie genug.
Wie je uns wieder anvertrauen
Dem Friedenshauche einer Flur,
Wenn Abendlicht und Morgengrauen
Befleckt sind mit der blutigen Spur?

Wenn in der Bäume gutem Raunen
Aufrauscht der Haß, der uns vertreibt!
Es lernten unsre Kinder staunen,
Warum man nicht zuhause bleibt?

Wir sind, mein Kind, nie mehr zuhause.
Vergiß das Wort, vergiß das Land
Und mach im Herzen eine Pause —
Dann gehn wir. Wohin? Unbekannt.

See just how your daughters nice,
Graceful, him who comes embrace!
With the guilty falls apace
Unmatched human sacrifice.

This earth bowed 'neath shame incurrèd
Has created its dictator.
And now drives the usurpator,
Austria to the German herd.

EMIGRANTS

Now we must part, from all things run
That were to us growth, childhood fair.
And we should e'en the language shun,
That words of our own hearts did bear.

The landscape will we leave behind,
That in its arms us tender bore.
For these woods we should hatred find,
Of which we always wanted more.

How e'er again can we confide
In peaceful breath of meadow place,
When morning's dawn and evening's light
Are sullied with the bloody trace?

When in trees whispers kind and good
Hate roars, that's driving us away!
To wonder learn our children would
At why at home we cannot stay.

We are, my child, no more at home.
Forget the word, the land forget,
And in your heart pause – ere we roam –
We'll go then. Where? Unknown as yet.

DIE DEUTSCHE SPRACHE

Daß ich bei Tag und Nacht
In dieser Sprache schreibe,
Ihr treuer als der Freundschaft und dem Weibe,
Es wird mir viel verdacht.

Ob, was ich sage, sie erröten macht,
Weil ich im zornigen Bescheide
Die Wahrheit nicht vermeide
Und nicht in fremde Tracht
Mein Herz verkleide:
Sie bleibt die alte doch in ihrer Pracht.

Hat sic mich leiden auch gemacht,
Ich tu ihr nichts zuleide.
Sie hat im Ausland oft die Nacht
Mit mir durchwacht,
Sie weiß, daß ich der Schurken keinen um die Macht,
Der sie geschändet, je beneide.

Wir tragen lieber unseres Unglücks Fracht
Und wirken, daß sie menschenwürdig bleibe.
Dann kommt sie, mich zu trösten sacht

Und wundert sich, wie ich es treibe,
Daß ich im Glauben, in der Hoffnung bleibe,
Obwohl ich weiter in ihr schreibe.

THE GERMAN LANGUAGE

That I both night and day
In this tongue writing spend,
More loyal to her than to wife or friend,
Men meet with much dismay.

If they are made to blush by what I say
Because in angry answer I
The truth do not deny
Nor in strange garb's array
My heart belie:
Th' old language she remains in rich display.

Though she's brought suffering my way,
To harm her I'd ne'er try.
Through nights in countries far away
With me she'd stay,
She knows that never envy scoundrels their great sway
Who violated her will I.

We'd rather let our sorrow on us weigh
And work to dignify her til the end.
She comes then, softly soothes my day
And is surprised how I things wend,
That I keep faith and hope until the end,
Though I time writing in her spend.

HELENE KAFKA*

SOLDATENLIED

Diese kunstlosen Ergüsse, die man kaum ein Gedicht nennen kann, verdienen dennoch in diese Sammlung einbezogen zu werden. Es ist einer gequälten Seele leidenschaftlicher Treueschwur für ihre Heimat, zu einer Zeit da Hitler's Armeen den größten Teil Europas erobert hatten und Österreichs Existenz als freies Land für immer zu Ende gekommen schien. Schwester Restituta, eine katholische Nonne, wußte, welches Schicksal sie mit ihrerm todesverachtenden Ausbruch heraufbeschwur. Sie wurde von einem "Volksgericht" zum Tode verurteilt und am 30. März 1943 hingerichtet. Ehre ihrem Angedenken!

Erwacht Soldaten und seid bereit, Gedenkt Eures ersten Eids
für das Land, in dem Ihr gelebt und geboren,
für Österreich habt Ihr alle geschworen.
Das sieht ja schon heute jedes Kind,
daß wir von den Preußen verraten sind.
Für die uralte heimische Tradition,
haben sie nichts als Spott und Hohn.
Den altösterreichischen General
kommandiert ein Gefreiter von dazumal.
Und der östreichische Rekrut
ist für sie nur als Kanonenfutter gut.
Zum beschimpfen und Leuteschinden
mögen sie andere Opfer finden.
Mit ihrem großen preußischen Maul
sind sie uns herabzusetzen nicht faul.
Dafür haben sie bis auf den letzten Rest
die Ostmarkzitrone ausgepreßt.
Unser Gold und Kunstschätze schleppten sie gleich
in ihr abgewirtschaftetes Nazireich.
Unser Fleisch, Obst, Milch und Butter
waren für sie ein willkommenes Futter.
Sie befreiten uns und ehe mans glaubt
hatten sie uns gänzlich ausgeraubt.

*Ordensname: Restituta

SOLDIER'S SONG

This artless effusion, which can hardly be called a poem, still deserves to be included in this collection. It is a tortured soul's passionate loyalty vow to her home country at a time when Hitler's armies had conquered most of Europe and when Austria's existence as an independent country seemed to have ended for all time. Sister Restituta, a Catholic nun, knew what fate she invited by her death-defying outburst. She was condemned to die by a "People's Court" and executed on March 30, 1943. Honor to her memory!

Awaken soldiers and be prepared, be mindful of your first oath
for the land in which you have lived and were born,
to Austria you've all loyalty sworn.
'Tis seen now by every child today,
that sorely the Prussians did us betray.
For the age-old tradition that's home-bred here
have they nothing but scorn and sneer.
The time-honored Austrian general
now takes orders from yesterday's corporal.
And so is the Austrian recruit
but good as cannon-fodder for them to shoot.
To revile and to ill-treat men
let them find other victims then.
With those great Prussian mouths that they own
they are not too lazy to tear us down.
But rather to the last drop they without doubt
have pressed the Ostmark lemon out.
Our gold and art treasures they carried away
to their mismanaged Nazi empire's decay.
Our butter, fruit, milk and meat,
these were all for them welcome food to eat.
Then they freed us and ere one could believe
they had robbed us and naught did they leave.

Selbst den ruhmvollen Namen stahl uns die Brut
und jetzt wollen sie auch noch unser Blut.
Der Bruder Schnürschuh ist nicht dumm,
gebt acht, er dreht die Gewehre um.
Der Tag der Vergeltung ist nicht mehr weit,
Soldaten gedenkt eures ersten Eids.
Österreich!
Wir Österreicher auf uns gestellt,
hatten Frieden und Freundschaft mit aller Welt.
Die Welt vergiftet mit ihrem Haß
Sie machet sich jedes Volk zum Feind.
Sie haben die Welt gegen sich vereint.
Die Mütter zittern, die Männer bangen,
der Himmel ist schwarz mit Wolken verhangen.
Der schrecklichste Krieg, den die Menschheit gekannt,
steht furchtbar vor unserm Heimatland. Es droht uns
Elend und Hungersnot, der Männer und Jünglinge Massentod,
Kameraden trotz dem verderblichen Wahn,
was gehen uns die Händel der Preußen an?
Was haben uns die Völker getan?
Wir nehmen die Waffen nur in die Hand
Im Kampf fürs freie Vaterland!

Too our glorious name from us stole the brood
and now they even yet desire our blood.
Dear Brother Lace-Shoe is no dunce,
look out, he will turn around the guns.
The vengeance day is not far anymore,
remember the oath, soldiers you first swore.
Austria!
We Austrians when left on our own
have with all of the world peace and friendship known.
The world that's poisoned with their hate
makes every nation its enemy.
They've gathered against them humanity.
The mothers tremble, men's hearts are failing
and cloudbanks of black are the heavens veiling.
The most frightful war known by mankind does stand
now awful before our native land. Us threaten
famine and misery, en masse men and youths dying terribly.
Comrades despite the deadly insanity,
what are the Prussians' affairs to you and me?
What has done to us humanity?
We'll only ever take weapons in hand
to fight for our free fatherland!

HANS JUST

WEIHNACHTEN

In Hitlers Kerkern 1941

Das ist ein Winter, den kein Christbaum schmückt.
Kein Heiland schläft im Stalle.
Verzweifle nicht, wenn bittre Not dich drückt.
Die Zeit ist hart für alle.

Ich denk' bei Tag und Nacht daran,
und mir tut's weh, daß ich nicht helfen kann.
Doch da kein Gott will seine Welt befrein,
muß ich und du und jeder Heiland sein.

DER MOND

Der Mond, der nächtens durch dein Fenster scheint,
schaut auch durch meins und sieht uns so vereint.

Und wandert deine Seele auf den Mond,
umarmt sie meine, die schon droben wohnt.

Der gute Mond, zu lindern ihren Schmerz,
drückt sie an sein gelassnes, kühles Herz.

CHRISTMAS

In Hitler's Dungeons 1941

'Tis winter that no Christmas tree can dress.
No Savior's in the stall.
Do not despair, when bitter cares you press
The times are hard for all.

Both night and day I think of it,
and me it hurts, that I can't help a bit.
Yet since no God intends his world to free,
must you and I, each one a Savior be.

THE MOON

The moon that nights will through your window glow
looks through mine too, sees us united so.

And if your soul up to the moon does fare,
'twill mine embrace, already dwelling there.

The kindly moon, to ease its sore distress
does it to his cool, patient bosom press.

JURA SOYFER

DACHAU-LIED

Stacheldraht, mit Tod geladen,
ist um unsre Welt gespannt.
Drauf ein Himmel ohne Gnaden
Sendet Frost und Sonnenbrand.
Fern von uns sind alle Freuden,
Fern die Heimat und die Fraun,
Wenn wir stumm zur Arbeit schreiten,
Tausende im Morgengraun.

Doch wir haben die Losung von Dachau gelernt
Und wir wurden stahlhart dabei.
Bleib ein Mensch, Kamerad,
Sei ein Mann, Kamerad,
Mach ganze Arbeit, pack an, Kamerad:
Denn Arbeit, denn Arbeit macht frei,
Denn Arbeit, denn Arbeit macht frei!*

Vor der Mündung der Gewehre
Leben wir bei Tag und Nacht.
Leben wird uns hier zur Lehre,
Schwerer, als wir's je gedacht.
Keiner mehr zählt Tag und Wochen,
Mancher schon die Jahre nicht.
Und so viele sind zerbrochen
Und verloren ihr Gesicht.

Doch wir haben die Losung von Dachau gelernt
Und wir wurden stahlhart dabei.
Bleib ein Mensch, Kamerad,
Sei ein Mann, Kamerad:
Mach ganze Arbeit, pack an, Kamerad
Denn Arbeit, denn Arbeit macht frei,
Denn Arbeit, denn Arbeit macht frei!

*Über dem Lagertor stand geschrieben: Arbeit macht frei!

SONG OF DACHAU

Barbed wire fences, harsh death bearing
Round our prison world here run.
Where a sky no mercy sharing
Sends the frost and burning sun.
Far from us abides all pleasure,
Homeland, wives are far away,
When to work mute steps we measure,
Thousands in the morning's gray.

But we've learned now the motto of Dachau by heart,
And hardened thus like steel are we.
Remain human, my friend,
Be a man now, my friend,
Complete your work and take hold here, my friend:
For work, for our work makes us free,
For work, for our work makes us free!*

In the face of guns we're living,
Day and night it is our lot.
Life to us its lesson giving
Harder than we ever thought.
Naught of days and weeks is spoken,
Many count no more each year.
And so many lives are broken,
And their faces lost in here.

But we've learned now the motto of Dachau by heart,
And thus hardened like steel are we.
Remain human, my friend,
Be a man now, my friend,
Complete your work and take hold here, my friend:
For work, for our work makes us free,
For work, for our work makes us free!

*Above the gate of the concentration camp was written: "Work makes us free."

Schlepp den Stein und zieh den Wagen,
keine Last sei dir zu schwer.
Der du warst in fernen Tagen,
bist du heut schon längst nicht mehr.
Stich den Spaten in die Erde,
grab dein Mitleid tief hinein
und im eignen Schweiße werde
selber du zu Stahl und Stein.

Doch wir haben die Losung von Dachau gelernt
Und wir wurden stahlhart dabei.
Bleib ein Mensch, Kamerad,
Sei ein Mann, Kamerad,
Mach ganze Arbeit, pack an, Kamerad:
Denn Arbeit, denn Arbeit macht frei,
Denn Arbeit, denn Arbeit macht frei!

Einst wird die Sirene künden:
Auf zum letzten Zählapell!
Draußen dann, wo wir uns finden,
bist du, Kamerad, zur Stell.
Hell wird uns die Freiheit lachen,
vorwärts geht's mit frischem Mut
und die Arbeit, die wir machen,
diese Arbeit, die wird gut!

Doch wir haben die Losung von Dachau gelernt
Und wir wurden stahlhart dabei.
Bleib ein Mensch, Kamerad,
Sei ein Mann, Kamerad,
Mach ganze Arbeit, pack an, Kamerad:
Denn Arbeit, denn Arbeit macht frei,
Denn Arbeit, denn Arbeit macht frei!

Haul stone, pull the van resistant,
Let naught drag you to your knees.
Who you were in days now distant
Long ago you ceased to be.
Dig your spade into the soil,
Bury pity that you feel,
And in your own sweat and toil
Turn yourself to stone and steel.

For we've learned now the motto of Dachau by heart,
And thus hardened like steel are we.
Remain human, my friend,
Be a man now, my friend,
Complete your work and take hold here, my friend:
For work, for our work makes us free,
For work, for our work makes us free!

Some day horns will call reminding:
Come, this rollcall marks the end!
When our place outside we're finding
You'll be with us there, my friend.
Bright will freedom smile, renewing,
On then with new heart and strength!
And the work that we are doing,
This work will be good at length.

For we've learned now the motto of Dachau by heart,
And thus hardened like steel are we.
Remain human, my friend,
Be a man now, my friend,
Complete your work and take hold here, my friend:
For work, for our work makes us free,
For work, for our work makes us free!

KÄTHE LEICHTER

AN MEINE BRÜDER

Bruder, schreckst auch du des Nachts empor aus wirren Träumen,
sind es Bilder, tags bewußt, die nachts den Schlaf umsäumen?
Warst du heute nacht bei Weib und Kind?
Ich war bei meinen Kindern. Deckte beide zu und sprach:
„Mutter kommt bald, brav sein und nicht weinen!"
Die Lampe warf ihr Licht auf Buch und Sofaecke,
wir saßen still, mein Mann und ich, daß nichts die Kinder wecke.
Da schreckt' ich auf, Fahl schien der Mond auf eiserne Gestelle.
Und da lieg ich unter vielen und doch so einsam und so kalt.
Ich in Ravensbrück, du in Sachsenhausen, in Dachau oder in Buchenwald.

Bruder, stehst du des Morgens frierend beim Appell?
Wir stehen stumm in Zehnerreihen, im Osten wird es langsam hell.
Steil ragt der Wald, wir atmen Luft in vollen Zügen,
Kräfte zu sammeln für den schweren Tag,
denn keiner von uns darf, will je unterliegen.
Da flammt's in Osten seltsam auf, als stünde die Welt in Flammen.
Wir nehmen es als gutes Zeichen. Bricht wirklich bald alles zusammen?
Und dann stehen wir stumm, nur die Fäuste geballt,
ich in Ravensbrück, du in Sachsenhausen, in Dachau oder in Buchenwald.

Bruder, stehst du auch des Tags mit der Schaufel in der Hand,
wird es nicht Mittag? Nimmt denn kein End' der Sand?
Oder schleppst auch du wie ich große schwere Steine?
Schmerzt auch dich der Rücken, brennen die Beine?
Sieh, du bist doch ein Mann, gewohnt an's harte Schlagen,
ich bin schwächer und mein Leib hat schon Kinder getragen.
Wie denkst du über unsrer Kinder Leben?
Werden Schläge, Strafblock, stets als Drohung schweben?
Und dann geht es weiter doch, im Herzen Hoffnung und Halt:
Ich in Ravensbrück, du in Sachsenhausen, in Dachau oder in Buchenwald.

TO MY BROTHERS

Brother, are you startled too at night from troubled dreaming,
are there daytime pictures that at night round sleep are streaming?
Have you been with wife and child tonight?
I was with my children. Covered both of them and said:
"Mother's coming soon, be good, no crying!"
The lamp on book and sofa corner threw its light,
my husband, I sat still that naught the children waken might.
I jerked awake. Pale shone the moon upon the iron bedstead.
And I'm lying there with many and yet so lonely and so cold.
I in Ravensbrück, you in Sachsenhausen, in Dachau or in Buchenwald.

Brother, do you at roll-call freeze by morning light?
We mutely stand in rows of ten, in the east the sky grows slowly bright.
The forest towers steep, we take deep breaths of air,
powers to gather for the grievous day,
to let ourselves succumb we must never dare.
Then in the east flames strangely rise as in world-wide conflagration.
We take it as a happy sign. Will all soon fall in disintegration?
And then we stand there mute, only holding our fists balled,
I in Ravensbrück, you in Sachsenhausen, in Dachau or in Buchenwald.

Brother, do you too stand all day with a shovel in your hand,
does not midday come? Is there no end to sand?
Or do you carry as I great and heavy stones?
Do your legs burn too, ache your back and bones?
See, you're a man and used to working hard and steady,
I am weaker and my body's borne children already.
What do you think about our children's life?
Will there always threaten blows and cell-block strife?
And it then continues, in our hearts hope and trust we hold:
I in Ravensbrück, you in Sachsenhausen, in Dachau or in Buchenwald.

Oh, Bruder, einmal kommt der Morgen, wo uns kein Appell mehr hält!
Wo weit offen die Tore, und vor uns liegt die große, die freie Welt.
Und dann werden wir KZler auf der breiten Straße wandern.
Doch auf uns warten noch die andern.
Und wer uns sieht, sieht die Furchen, die das Leid uns in das Antlitz geschrieben,
sieht Spuren von Körper- und Seelenqualen, die uns ein bleibendes Mal geblieben.
Und wer uns sieht, sieht den Zorn, der hell in unseren Augen blitzt,
sieht den jauchzenden Freiheitsjubel, der ganz unsere Herzen besitzt.
Und dann reihen wir uns ein, in die letzte große Kolonne,
dann heißt es zum letzten Male: Vorwärts, marsch!
Und jetzt führt der Weg zum Licht und zur Sonne.
Oh, Bruder, siehst du gleich mir diesen Tag, du mußt doch denken: Er kommt bald!
Und dann ziehen wir aus Ravensbrück, aus Sachsenhausen, aus Dachau und aus Buchenwald.

Oh Brother, someday comes the morning when roll-calls hold us no more!
When before us the great, grand, free world lies, and wide open is the door.
And then will all we prisoners walk streets that are broad and straight.
But for us still the others wait.
And who sees us sees the wrinkles that pain and suffering wrote in our faces,
sees permanent marks of the suffering that on body and soul left its traces.
And who sees us sees the angry rage that in our eyes flashes bright,
sees the jubilant joy of freedom that possesses our hearts with its might.
And then we'll line up in the great column, the very last one,
then call for the final time: Forward, march!
And now leads the way to light and the sun.
Oh Brother, you must think: It comes soon!, If like me you're by that day enthralled.
And then we will come from Ravensbrück, from Sachenshausen, from Dachau and from Buchenwald.

PAULA VON PRERADOVIĆ

WIENER REIMCHRONIK, 1945

I. DER ABSTAND

Deinem Blick zieht sich ein Schleier vor,
Viel zu bang bist du, um auszusagen,
Siehst du's brennen wie zu Neros Tagen,
Hörst du's donnern schauerlich ans Tor;

Stehst du eingemauert in die Not,
Packt die Angst dich an mit Drachenkrallen,
Spürst du die Geschosse sausend fallen,
Liegt zu deinen Füßen einer tot.

Stumm erträgst du, steinernen Gesichts,
Was du nur aus Sagenbüchern kanntest,
Eine ferne Vorzeit-Fabel nanntest.
Stumm erträgst du's, und du kündest nichts.

Eines ungeheuren Schicksals Drohn
Läßt du dir vom Alltag leise lindern.
Da der Schlachtlärm brüllt, spielst du mit Kindern,
Issest ruhig deine Nachtration.

Aber da dich forttrug nur *ein* Schritt,
Baut sich das Entsetzen auf zu Bildern,
Und du wagst in Worten abzuschildern,
Was dein Herz an Unerhörtem litt.

II. FLIEGERALARM

Ängstlich achtend auf den Stundenschlag,
Siehst du durch die Gassen bang dich laufen,
Rüben, Magermilch und Brot zu kaufen;
Über Wien der fahle Vormittag.

CHRONICLE IN VERSE, VIENNA 1945

I. PERSPECTIVE

What you darkly see you cannot state,
Much too terrified to be a hero:
See the fires set by another Nero
Hear the fearful thundering at the gate.

There you stand, immured in your distress,
Clutched by dragon claws of fear appalling,
All around the hissing bullets falling,
At your feet a body lies, lifeless.

Speechless witness, with a face of stone,
You see tales of ancient strife
Myths from books, come back to life,
Speechless you stand up to this, alone.

Feeling threatened by a monstrous fate
You allow routine to soothe your day
Battles rage, you watch the children play,
Share your rations, let them stay up late.

Yet a single step beyond, in time,
Even horror seeks and finds a form,
Words can make a net to catch a storm,
Your heart's anguish can be told in rhyme.

II. AIR RAID ALARM

Heeding anxiously the church clock's tale,
See yourself afraid through alleys flying,
Turnips, bread and skim milk swiftly buying;
O'er Vienna morning faded, pale.

Rasch noch hier hinein um Salz und Quark.
Weh, es wird von Süden angeflogen?
Und aus fremdem Munde, schreckverzogen,
Kreischt es heiser: „Kärnten, Steiermark!"

Nur nach Haus, so schnell der Fuß dich trägt.
Und indes du stürmst die Treppenstufen,
Gellt's dich an: „Der Kuckuck hat gerufen!"
Und du weißt nicht, ob dein Puls noch schlägt.

Voll Gerenne ist das ganze Haus.
Ja, ihr müßt euch eilends fertigmachen,
In den Keller mit den Siebensachen,
Und ich hänge noch die Fenster aus.

Doch da heult auch schon wie Höllenhohn,
Jeden Nerv mit Urweltgrauen füllend,
Wie aus Saurierrachen endlos brüllend,
Sinkend, schwellend der Sirene Ton.

III. LUFTANGRIFF

Silberhelle Todesvögelschar,
Grausam schön durch Gottes Himmel reigend,
Mit diamantner Drohung übersteigend
Alles, was seit alters furchtbar war:

Keiner sieht der lichten Flüge Pracht,
Denn es hockt in Katakombendunkel,
Denn es horcht bei ängstlichem Gemunkel
Eng das Volk in feuchter Kellernacht;

Hört nur kreisenden Motorenlaut
Ob den festen Mauern schwirrend tönen,
Spürt die fromme Erde zitternd dröhnen,
Drauf die Väter einst die Stadt erbaut.

Quickly yet for salt and curds in here.
Woe, from south they fly in, it's reported?
And a stranger shrieks with words distorted:
"Styria, Carinthia!" in fear.

Home now just as fast as foot will bear.
And then as you up the stairs come bounding,
In your ears "The coocoo called!" is pounding,
You know not if your pulse still beats there.

Now commotion all the house does fill.
Yes, you must get ready in a hurry,
To the cellar with belongings scurry,
And I must remove the window still.

Howls already now like hell's disdain
Each nerve with primeval terror filling
As from saurian throat now endless shrilling,
Sinking, swelling siren tones again.

III. AIR RAID

Death bird flock with brightly silver sheen,
Fiercely lovely dance through God's sky leading,
There with diamond menace far exceeding
All that has for ages frightful been:

None can see the glory of bright flight,
For there crouch in grave-like darkness queasy,
For there hearken mid the talk uneasy,
Close the people in damp cellar night;

Hear the engine tones now circle on,
O'er the solid walls their hum is sounding,
Feel the pious trembling earth resounding,
Which the fathers built the town upon.

Und nach vieler Stunden Angst und Frost,
Ekler Pferchung in den nächtig-nassen
Untergründen endlich freigelassen,
Heimgegeben an der Sonne Trost,

Sehn sie breiter Brände Grau und Rot
Gassenauf den Winterhimmel färben,
Sehn sie neue Trümmer, neues Sterben,
Und sie wünschen selbst, sie wären tot.

IV. FRAUENGEFÄNGNIS DER GESTAPO

Schmaler Kerkerhof im Abendlicht,
Und im Hof ein Baum in Knospenfülle.
Heute sprengen sie die braune Hülle.
Schwestern, starrt so trüb durchs Gitter nicht!

Hört den nahen tiefen Glockenton.
Wußtet ihr's? Es ist Karsamstag heute.
Draußen gehen feierlich die Leute
Jetzt zur Auferstehungsprozession.

Weint nicht, Schwestern! Singt das Freiheitslied!
Singt in trotzig vollen, wilden Chören,
Daß die Männer überm Hof uns hören,
Und aus allen Zellen singt man mit.

Heute stellen sich die Wächter taub.
Ostern ist. Sie werden uns nicht strafen.
Schwestern, legt euch voller Hoffnung schlafen.
Morgen früh steht unser Baum in Laub.

In der späten Nacht schärft euer Ohr.
Mörser hört ihr dröhnen fern aus Süden.
Fürchtet nichts mehr! Rastet eure müden
Leiber aus. Bald öffnet sich das Tor.

After many hours of frost and fear,
Crammed in loathsome damp night, them concealing
Underground, then freed at last, revealing
Faces to the sunlight's comfort dear,

See they up the streets: broad, gray and red,
Painting winter's sky the burnings flying,
Ruins new they see, and much new dying,
And they wish that they themselves were dead.

IV. WOMEN'S PRISON OF THE GESTAPO

Narrow prison court in twilight there,
In the court a tree, its buds embracing.
And today each bursts from its brown casing.
Sisters, don't through bars so sadly stare!

Hear the near deep bell tones as they're made.
Ringing Easter Eve now from the steeple.
Out there festively go all the people
To the resurrection's gay parade.

Weep not, sisters! Sing the freedom song!
Sing in full, in wild defiant chorus,
That men o'er the court may not ignore us,
And from all the cells they sing along.

Watchmen act as though they're deaf today,
Punish not. It's Easter's celebration.
Sisters, lie down full of expectation.
In the morn our tree will leaves display.

Late at night then open wide your ear.
Mortars from far south you will hear rumbling.
Fear no more! Rest out your weary, stumbling
Bodies. Soon the gate will open here.

V. SCHLACHT

Wieder in der Erde finstrem Bauch
Haust das Volk auf Pritschen, eng geschichtet,
Kocht das Volk an Feuern, schnell errichtet,
Atmet es in Feuchte, Stank und Rauch.

Stalinorgel heult und pfaucht und singt.
O du Frühlingstag, vom Kampf geschändet!
Wann denn wird das Elend abgewendet?
In die Häuser schon der Fremde dringt.

In des Gartens Unschuld fällt das Blei.
Letzte Fensterscheiben splittern klirrend.
Immer wieder, durch die Lüfte schwirrend,
Fährt ein pfeifendes Geschoß vorbei.

Auf der Straße zweie, Frau und Mann.
Schrei und Stürzen. Tragt sie in die Kammer!
Wie sie bluten. Auswegloser Jammer!
Nichts und niemand, der sie retten kann.

Morphium! – Wasser! – Wildes Menschenweh! –
Da die Mörser für Minuten schweigen,
Hörst du in den reinen Himmel steigen
Einer Meise süßes Tsi-tsi-be.

VI. DER DOM

Hoher Dom, du starkes Herz der Stadt,
Ach, wer weiß noch, wie bei Frührots Scheinen
In der satten Glut von Edelsteinen
Bunt das Licht in dir gejubelt hat?

Wer noch weiß es, wie von deinem Turm,
Deinem einen, einzigen, die tiefen,
Angestammten Glocken singend riefen,
Erzen brandend als ein heiliger Sturm?

V. BATTLE

In the earth's dark belly once again
Packed together folk on guard beds dwelling,
Cook on quick laid fires so evil smelling,
Breathing where but smoke and dampness reign.

Stalin organ howls and puffs and hums.
O spring day, by battle desecrated!
When will this misfortune have abated?
Into houses now the stranger comes.

Lead falls in the garden innocent.
Final window panes in shards are crashing.
E'er repeating, through the breezes dashing,
Whistle of a bullet not yet spent.

On the street a couple: woman, man.
Scream, collapse. Them to the chamber carry!
How they bleed. Escapeless woe will tarry!
None who's here can save them, nothing can.

Morphium! – Water! – Savage human pain!
When for minutes mortars cease their pounding,
You hear in the pure clear sky resounding,
Rising sweet a titmouse's refrain.

VI. THE CATHEDRAL

High cathedral, city's heart so strong,
Ah, who still knows how in dawn's red glowing
In the sated fire of jewels flowing
Gay the light in you exulted long?

Who still knows how from your tow'ring form,
From your one and only spire, the ringing
Deep ancestral bells all called out singing,
Breaking brazen waves in holy storm?

Ach, unsäglich standest du uns da,
Steines Hochzeit, Säulenwald des Heiles,
Maßwerks Wunder, Schwung des Gottespfeiles,
Über mächtigen Daches Gloria.

Eines Abends aber stiegest du,
So, als wolltst du eine Fackel werden,
Funkenübersprüht, von Flammenherden
Eingeglüht, den kühlen Sternen zu.

Standest feurig leuchtend in der Nacht,
Deine Stadt noch einmal überkrönend,
Liebevoll ihr Unglück noch verschönend,
Und dann fielst du in der Frühlingsschlacht.

How immense you stood there for us, ah!
Stony wedding, pillars of salvation,
God's arched chamber, wondrous trace-creation
Over mighty ceiling's gloria.

But one night you climbed aloft as though
You desired to be a flambeau lighted,
Sprayed with sparks, by flaming hearths ignited,
Toward cool distant stars you rose aglow.

Stood there fiery brilliant in the night,
Over-crowned your town again while dying,
Lovingly its woe still beautifying,
And you fell then in the springtime fight.

THEODOR KRAMER

DER OFEN VON LUBLIN

Es steht ein Ofen, ein seltsamer Schacht,
ins Sandfeld gebaut, bei Lublin;
es führten die Züge bei Tag und bei Nacht
das Röstgut in Viehwagen hin.
Es wurden viel Menschen aus jeglichem Land
vergast und auch noch lebendig verbrannt
im feurigen Schacht von Lublin.

Die flattern ließen drei Jahre am Mast
ihr Hakenkreuz über Lublin,
sie trieb beim Verscharren nicht ängstliche Hast,
hier galt es noch Nutzen zu ziehn.
Es wurde die Asche der Knochen sortiert,
in jutene Säcke gefüllt und plombiert
als Dünger geführt aus Lublin.

Nun flattert der fünffach gezackte Stern
im Sommerwind über Lublin.
Der Schacht ist erkaltet; doch nahe und fern
legt Schwalch auf die Länder sich hin,
und fortfrißt, solang nicht vom Henkerbeil fällt
des letzten Schinderknechts Haupt, an der Welt
die feurige Schmach von Lublin.

THE OVEN OF LUBLIN

There stands an oven, a strange shaft to see,
'twas built in the sand near Lublin;
the trains day and night brought continuously
in cattle cars goods to put in.
And people from every land did arrive,
were gassed and were even burned up alive
in the fiery hot pit of Lublin.

They who from flagpoles let wave for three years
their swastika over Lublin
to bury in haste were not driven by fears,
for there was still profit to win.
The ashes of bones were sifted, concealed
and filled into sacks made of jute which were sealed
and carried as dung from Lublin.

Now fluttering flies the five-pointed star
in summer's wind over Lublin.
The shaft has grown cold; and yet still near and far
the oven's old glow nestles in.
And eats at the world, til the axe its last head
has claimed and knacker's last knave is dead,
the fiery disgrace of Lublin.

ILSE WEBER

WEG NACH THERESIENSTADT

Das ist der Weg nach Theresienstadt,
Den Tausende mühsam beschritten,
Und jeder von all den Tausenden hat
Das gleiche Unrecht erlitten.
Sie gingen ihn mit gesenktem Haupt,
Den Zionsstern über dem Herzen,
Die müden Füße wund und bestaubt,
Die Seelen zerquält von Schmerzen.
Von schwerer Bürde zerschunden die Hand,
Getrieben von rauhen Befehlen,
Oh, endloser Weg im Sonnenbrand,
Mit durstgepeinigten Kehlen.
Das ist der Weg nach Theresienstadt,
Der unser Herzblut getrunken,
Wo sterbend hier auf dem steinigen Pfad
Manch müder Greis gesunken.
Es ist ein Weg voller Elend und Grauen,
Wo Ströme von Tränen geflossen,
Die klagende Kinder und stöhnende Frauen
In hilflosem Jammer vergossen.
Hier wankten Greise mit irrem Blick,
Im ergebenen Trott der Herde,
Wieviele gehn nie mehr den Weg zurück,
Denn gnädig umschließt sie die Erde.
Das ist auch der Weg, den hinab mit Hast
Laut dröhnend rollten die Wagen,
Die unablässig die ächzende Last,
Die Totgeweihten getragen,
Das ist der Weg nach Theresienstadt,
Mit Leiden ungemessen,
Und wer ihn einmal gesehen hat,
Der wird ihn nie mehr vergessen.

THE ROAD TO TEREZIN

That is the way toward Terezin town
That thousands did struggle along,
And each among all of the ones who went down
Did suffer the selfsame wrong.
With heads bowed low they traveled that street,
The Zion's star over each heart,
With weary and sore and dusty feet
And spirits racked with the smart.
With hand that the heavy burden did flay,
Pressed on by commands roughly cursed,
Neath burning sun, oh infinite way,
With throats that were parched with thirst.
That is the way toward Terezin town,
The one that our hearts' blood drank,
Where dying here on the path's rocky crown
Many an old man sank.
It is a way full of wretchedness, dread,
Where torrents of tears flowing free
By suffering children and women were shed
In helpless abject misery.
Here old men reeled with gaze gone astray
In submissive trot of the herd.
How many will never come back this way,
For mercifully they are interred.
'Tis too the way down which with haste unslowed
The rolling trucks loudly boomed,
That unrelenting the creaking load
Did bear, the ones who were doomed.
That is the way toward Terezin town
With its unmeasured pain,
And who has it seen and who has it known
Will never forget it again.

PAUL CELAN

TODESFUGE

Schwarze Milch der Frühe wir trinken sie abends
wir trinken sie mittags und morgens wir trinken sie nachts
wir trinken und trinken
wir schaufeln ein Grab in den Lüften da liegt man nicht eng
Ein Mann wohnt im Haus der spielt mit den Schlangen der schreibt
der schreibt wenn es dunkelt nach Deutschland dein goldenes Haar
  Margarete
er schreibt es und tritt vor das Haus und es blitzen die Sterne er pfeift seine
  Rüden herbei
er pfeift seine Juden hervor läßt schaufeln ein Grab in der Erde
er befiehlt uns spielt auf nun zum Tanz

Schwarze Milch der Frühe wir trinken dich nachts
wir trinken dich morgens und mittags wir trinken dich abends
wir trinken und trinken
Ein Mann wohnt im Haus der spielt mit den Schlangen der schreibt
der schreibt wenn es dunkelt nach Deutschland dein goldenes Haar
  Margarete
Dein aschenes Haar Sulamith wir schaufeln ein Grab in den Lüften da
  liegt man nicht eng

Er ruft stecht tiefer ins Erdreich ihr einen ihr andern singet und spielt
er greift nach dem Eisen im Gurt er schwingts seine Augen sind blau
stecht tiefer die Spaten ihr einen ihr andern spielt weiter zum Tanz auf

Schwarze Milch der Frühe wir trinken dich nachts
wir trinken dich mittags und morgens wir trinken dich abends
wir trinken und trinken
ein Mann wohnt Haus dein goldenes Haar Margarete
dein aschenes Haar Sulamith er spielt mit den Schlangen

Er ruft spielt süßer den Tod der Tod ist ein Meister aus Deutschland
er ruft streicht dunkler die Geigen dann steigt ihr als Rauch in die Luft
dann habt ihr ein Grab in den Wolken da liegt man nicht eng

DEATH FUGUE

Black milk of daybreak we drink it at sundown
we drink it at noon in the morning we drink it at night
we drink and we drink it
we dig a grave in the breezes there one lies unconfined
A man lives in the house he plays with the serpents he writes
he writes when dusk falls to Germany your golden hair Margarete
he writes it and steps out of doors and the stars are flashing he whistles his pack out
he whistles his Jews out in earth has them dig for a grave
he commands us strike up for the dance

Black milk of daybreak we drink you at night
we drink in the morning at noon we drink you at sundown
we drink and we drink you
A man lives in the house he plays with the serpents he writes
he writes when dusk falls to Germany your golden hair Margarete
your ashen hair Shulamith we dig a grave in the breezes there one lies unconfined.

He calls out jab deeper into the earth you lot you others sing now and play
he grabs at the iron in his belt he waves it his eyes are blue
jab deeper you lot with your spades you others play on for the dance

Black milk of daybreak we drink you at night
we drink you at noon in the morning we drink you at sundown
we drink and we drink you
a man lives in the house your golden hair Margarete
your ashen hair Shulamith he plays with the serpents

He calls out more sweetly play death death is a master from Germany
he calls out more darkly now stroke your strings then as smoke you will rise into air
then a grave you will have in the clouds there one lies unconfined

Schwarze Milch der Frühe wir trinken dich nachts
wir trinken dich mittags der Tod ist ein Meister aus Deutschland
wir trinken dich abends und morgens wir trinken und trinken
der Tod ist ein Meister aus Deutschland sein Auge ist blau
er trifft dich mit bleierner Kugel er trifft dich genau
ein Mann wohnt im Haus dein goldenes Haar Margarete
er hetzt seine Rüden auf uns er schenkt uns ein Grab in der Luft
er spielt mit den Schlangen und träumet der Tod ist ein Meister aus
 Deutschland

dein goldenes Haar Margarete
dein aschenes Haar Sulamith

Black milk of daybreak we drink you at night
we drink you at noon death is a master from Germany
we drink you at sundown and in the morning we drink and we drink you
death is a master from Germany his eyes are blue
he strikes you with leaden bullets his aim is true
a man lives in the house your golden hair Margarete
he sets his pack on to us he grants us a grave in the air
he plays with the serpents and daydreams death is a master from Germany

your golden hair Margarete
your ashen hair Shulamith

ERNST WALDINGER

DER FALSCHE PROPHET

> In deinen Häusern wirst du wohnen wie zuvor.
> (Josef Weinheber)

In deinen Häusern wirst du wohnen wie zuvor,
So sprachst du, dein und ihrer schamlos spottend.
Du brauchtest des Psalmisten Ton und Wort
In jener Stunde, da sein altes Volk
Aus Häusern, drin sie tausend Jahre saßen
Von jenen, denen du den Hüttenfrieden,
Den Frieden des Milleniums versprachst,
Vertrieben ward, so daß der bittre Satz
Vom Menschensohn, der keine Bleibe hat,
Im Reiche der Barbaren wieder wahr ward.

In deinen Häusern wirst du wohnen wie zuvor,
So sprachst du, da der Wurm am Holz schon fraß,
Da schon die Vögel der Vernichtung flogen
Und Eisendung, der die Verwesung birgt,
In fernen Ländern fleißig niederwarfen,
In allen Händen allenthalb die Hämmer
Schon an den Todessensen rege waren.

In deinen Häusern wirst du wohnen wie zuvor . . .
In deinem wohnst du freilich längst nicht mehr,
Denn als die Flamme fiel, die Rächer nahten,
Da zogest du das schmale Erdgeviert,
Das unser aller Wohnung sein wird, vor.
Du wußtest wohl, daß das, was du versprachst,
Prophet, dem Meister aller Lügen folgend,
Nur Schutt und Trümmer, nicht den Hüttenfrieden,
Den Frieden des Milleniums enthielt.
Wir aber glauben, daß ein neuer Morgen,
Ein Morgen aus betauter Stille steigend,
Bereits im Zwielicht unsres Fensters steht,
Daß aus den grünen Ähren, aus den Wiesen
In bleicher Frühe, aus dem Wälderdunkel,
So drohend aufgereckt, der Friede flüstert.

THE FALSE PROPHET

> In your own houses you'll dwell as before.
> (Josef Weinheber)

You'll dwell in your own houses as you did before,
You said it, mocking yourself and them so shameless.
You utilized the psalmist's tone and word
In that same moment when his ancient folk
From homes where they a thousand years resided
By those to whom you pledged peace in the cottage,
The lasting peace of the millenium,
Were driven out, so that the bitter tale
Of Son of Man who has no place to stay
Once more was true in that barbaric empire.

You'll dwell in your own houses as you did before,
You said it, worms already gnawed the wood,
Destruction's birds already then were flying,
Were hard at work at dropping iron dung
That holds decay in store, in foreign countries,
In every hand on every side the hammers
Were busy whetting scythes of death already.

You'll dwell in your own houses as you did before . . .
'Tis long, of course, since in your own you dwelt,
For when the blazes fell, avengers nearing,
Then you preferred the narrow piece of earth
That for us all a dwelling once will be.
You knew full well that that which you had pledged,
When Master of All Lies you followed, Prophet,
But rubble and debris, not peace in cottage,
The peace of the millenium contained.
But we believe that now a bright new morning,
A morning rising from a dewy stillness,
Already in our window's gloaming stands,
That from the verdant ears and from the meadows
In pallid morning, from the forest's darkness,
So menacingly raised, peace softly whispers.

SIE HABEN UNSER HEIMWEH GETÖTET!

Schneeberge, fern, wie oft sie uns verschwammen
Im Dunste wie in trübem Spiegelglas!
Gelangs nicht so die Heimat zu verschlammen
Dem Geist der Zeit, der wie ein böses Gas,
Zersetzend alles, aus den Sümpfen steigt,
Die Mord und Mordsucht zwischen den Ruinen
In Lachen hinterliessen – ach, es schweigt
Das Edle; bitter, stumm sind die ihm dienen.

Den Duft der brachen Scholle wehts im März
Herüber noch, doch wird Erinnrung müder,
Schlägt sich ein Brandgeruch auf unser Herz,
Gemahnend an die Marter unsrer Brüder.
Sie haben uns hierher gejagt, sie leiden
Das Los nun, das sie sich heraufbeschworen –
Daß wir entkamen, ist, was sie uns neiden:
Es zischt ihr Lästerwort in unsern Ohren.

Schneeberge, fern, ihr sollt uns nie verschwimmen,
Wischt das Gedächtnis nur den Spiegel rein;
Der Kinderwald im Glanz der Vogelstimmen
Wird immerdar in unsrer Seele sein.
Und haben sie das Heimweh uns getötet,
Sind wir nun Bürger neuer Heimatwelt,
Die alte bleibt, vom Flammenschein umrötet
Die Mutter, die uns still im Schoße hält.

VON DER LIEBE ZUR HEIMAT

Nach Recht und Unrecht fragt die Liebe nie:
Die Heimat is wie eine Melodie,
Ein Ammenlied, ins Herz dir eingesungen –
Du nahst im Geist ihr wie der Mutter Knie,
Das deine Kinderarme einst umschlungen.

THEY KILLED OUR LONGING FOR OUR HOMELAND

How oft the distant mountains capped with snow
Grew blurred as in a clouded mirror's glass!
Did not its filth thus o'er the homeland sow
This era's spirit, that, like some foul gas,
Dissolving all, climbs from the swamps at will,
Which left behind among the ruins there
In puddles murder, bloodthirst – oh, grown still
What's noble; mute its servants in despair.

In March still blows the scent of fallow land
O'er to us, yet recall becomes more weary,
When smell of fire our heart beleagers and
Of martyred brothers gives reminder dreary.
They drove us hither and they suffer now
The fate that they called forth with all its fears –
That we escaped is what they'd disallow:
Their blasphemies are hissing in our ears.

You distant snow-capped hills should ne'er grow blurred,
If memory but wipes the mirror clean;
The childhood woods aglow with voice of bird
Will e'er be in our soul where they have been.
Though homesickness has been killed by the foe,
Though we belong now to a new home world,
The old remains, flame-wrapped in fiery glow,
The mother in whose lap we still are curled.

ON LOVE OF THE HOMELAND

Love never asks what right and wrong may be:
The homeland is so like a melody,
A nanny's song, into your heart once sung –
Your spirit nears it like the mother's knee
To which your arms in childhood tightly clung.

Nach Recht und Unrecht fragt die Liebe nie,
Und welcher Schuld man auch die Menschen zieh,
Kains Söhne, die zum Brudermord gedungen;
Die Heimat, die dir Wort und Seele lieh,
Du atmest sie wie Bergluft in die Lungen.

Geruhsam geht der Fluß und grast das Vieh;
Lausch' inniger und hingegebner, sieh:
Grün strahlt das Land und spricht mit stillen Zungen.
Nach Recht und Unrecht fragt die Liebe nie,
Den Trost hast du dem Unheil abgerungen.

VERZEIHEN, ABER NICHT VERGESSEN

Dünkt's mich auch übermenschlich, doch verzeihn
Muß ich am Ende; ich verzeih nicht gern!
Die Rache, lehrt die Schrift, gebührt dem Herrn.
Wir müssen uns dem Werk der Liebe weihn.

Doch hör ich noch das Hilfeschrein
Der Brüer drüben mit dem Davidstern;
In meine Träume sickert noch von fern
Der Brandgeruch, ich seh den Feuerschein

Fast nahe noch, der aus den hundert Essen,
In die sie meine Schwestern warfen, schwelt . . .
Wag's, Richter, hier zu wägen und zu messen!

Verflucht, wer eins der Opfer nur verhehlt!
Unmenschlich wär ich, wollt ich sie vergessen,
So herzlos wie ein Stein, so unbeseelt!

Love never asks what right and wrong may be,
Whatever guilt one may in people see,
Cain's sons, engaged to murder brothers young;
The home that gave you word and spirit free,
You breathe like mountain air into your lungs.

The cattle graze, the stream flows peacefully;
More heartfelt, more devoted listen, see:
Green grows the land and speaks with quiet tongue.
Love never asks what right or wrong may be,
From trouble you've that consolation won.

FORGIVE, BUT DO NOT FORGET

Though it seems superhuman, but at last
I must forgive: it is no glad-done deed.
Vengeance is for the Lord (so says our creed),
But we must pledge ourselves to loving's task.

Yet from that place I still can hear the cry
of brothers who were marked with David's star,
And through my dreams there still seeps from afar
The burning smell: I see, as though nearby,

The fires, within a hundred ovens lit,
Those where my sisters were all thrown . . .
Dare, judge, to weigh the deed or measure it!

Cursèd be he who cedes oblivion
A single victim; were I to forget,
I'd be inhuman, just like soulless stone.

DIE MAHNMALE

Dem Andenken meiner Schwiegermutter Paula Winternitz-Freud

Gedenk ich euer, die die Schergen täglich
Wie Vieh zur Schlachtbank in die Lager trieben,
Klag ich mich an, daß es ins Herz geschrieben
Nicht mehr uns ist, daß das, was so unsäglich

Als Schrecken damals wach war, schwach und kläglich
Uns im Gedächtnis lebt . . . Mahnmale blieben
Mit leeren Namen der Millionen Lieben –
Unfaßbar schien es einst und unerträglich.

Gibt uns ein Stein nur die Entsetzenskunde?
Was sagt er aus von ihrer letzten Nacht,
Die sie, in die Waggons gepfercht, durchwacht?

Was weiß er schon von ihrer letzten Stunde,
Bevor sie starben, stöhnend oder stumm,
Von ihrem sinnlosen Martyrium?

PAPST JOHANNES XXIII

In hora mortis

Du Menschlichster, den ich nicht anerkenne,
Ich bin ein Jude und vielleicht ein Heide,
Doch dessen Namen ich mit Ehrfurcht nenne,
Du Heiliger in deinem Ruhm und Leide,
Vom „untern Berg" du Bauernsohn und Senne,
O folgte dir die Herde auf die Weide,
Dir Sterbendem, wieviel die Welt gewänne:
Denn ewig blieb das Kriegsschwert in der Scheide.

THE MEMORIALS

In memory of my mother-in-law Paula Winternitz-Freud

When I recall you whom the henchmen sent
Like cattle to the slaughter day by day,
I blame myself that in our hearts today
It's not inscribed, that that which terror meant

Beyond all words, but weakly evident
Within our memory lives – memorials stay
That empty names of millions loved display –
't once seemed we could not bear it, comprehend.

Does but a stone us horror's record show?
What does it say about their night, the last
That they while packed in boxcars waking passed?

What does it really of their last hour know,
Before they perished, moaning or yet dumb,
The victims of a senseless martyrdom?

POPE JOHN XXIII

In hora mortis

You whom I disavow, most human one,
I am a Jew, and heathen I may be,
Whose name with awe to speak I've yet begun,
You saint in both your fame and misery,
From "neath the mount" you herdsman, peasant's son,
If, dying man, would heed you on the lea
The flock, how much would for the world be won:
For sheathed would be war's sword eternally.

ICH BIN EIN SOHN DER DEUTSCHEN SPRACHE

Wenn ich auch nicht die alten Psalmen summ,
Ich wandle auf der Ahnen Tränenspur;
Ich fühl mich eins mit aller Kreatur,
In welcher Maske sie sich auch vermumm.

Tod tobt aus jenen – und der Tod ist stumm;
Es schrillen Schrei und roher Racheschwur –
Ich bin ein Sohn der deutschen Sprache nur,
Ich bin kein Deutscher, wohl ist mir darum.

Ich bin ein Sohn der deutschen Sprache nur;
Was meinem Volk an Leid auch widerfuhr,
In meinem Worte klärt sich's und beweist

Mein Judenblut und daß der Menschengeist
Der stärkre ist – : aus vielen finstern Stunden
Hab' ich zum Licht des Liedes heimgefunden.

I AM A SON OF THE GERMAN LANGUAGE

Though I hum not a psalm's old wonted air,
I walk the father's path of tears; revere
And feel I'm one with every creature here,
Whatever mask it might elect to wear.

Death roars from those – and death is silent there;
We shrieking screams, raw oaths of vengeance here –
A son am I of German language sheer,
I am no German, well in that I fare.

A son am I of German language pure;
What'er my folk of sorrow did endure,
In my own word reveals itself and shows

My Jewish blood, that man's heart is of those
The stronger one –: from hours of darkest night
I've found my way home to the poem's light.

BERICHT AUS DEUTSCHLAND, 1944

Nun naht des Reiches allerletzte Stunde;
Fast ging die ganze Welt an ihm zu Grunde;
Das Land durchziehn nun – schauerliche Kunde! –
Die Rattenheere und die tollen Hunde.

Die Rattenheere und die tollen Hunde;
Vampyr und Werwolf waren hier im Bunde;
Der Blutwahn röchelt, Geifer vor dem Munde.
Ob je die Welt von solchem Gift gesunde?

Es soll nach überheblichem Befunde
Die Welt – unheilbare Amfortaswunde! –
An Deutschland einst genesen . . . ihre Runde
Ziehn Rattenheere und die tollen Hunde.

Die Rattenheere und die tollen Hunde!
Das wühlt im Schutt! Mit wohlgewognem Pfunde
Zahlt nun das Reich die Schuld dem Höllenschlunde;
Der Geist ertrank in Schmach, in Schmutz, im Schunde.

REPORT FROM GERMANY, 1944

And now the Reich's last hour is coming round;
It nearly brought the world down to the ground;
What ghastliness! – now through the land are bound
The rats in armies and the rabid hounds.

The rats in armies and the rabid hounds;
Vampire and werewolf were together bound;
The bloodthirst slavers, makes a gasping sound.
Can earth e'er from such venom free be found?

One day, so says what's haughtily been found,
The world – incurable Amfortas-wound! –
Through Germany will convalesce – their round
Make rats in armies and the rabid hounds.

The rats in armies and the rabid hounds!
They dig in ruins! And with well weighed pound
Hell's jaws its debt the Reich is paying found;
In shame, in filth, in trash the spirit drowned.

GERTRUD FUSSENEGGER

WIE WEIT...

Wie weit
wie weit seid ihr uns vorausgegangen
Brüder, Söhne, Freunde,
wie weit
in die Nacht!

Wir nennen
eure Namen noch immer
aber die Spur
eurer Schritte, wo ist sie?
Andere
sind gekommen
haben den schmalen Pfad
den ihr getreten
eingeebnet und ausgelöscht.
Andere
sind an eueren Tischen gesessen
andere
haben euere Kinder
als Väter belehrt.

Die Nächte der Tränen
für euch verweint
sie sind vorüber
versickert ins Morgengrauen
nüchterner Tage.
Die Klaue des Schmerzes
die uns zerfleischte
euretwillen
damals und lange
sie ließ uns los.
Wir lernten leben
mit euerem Tode
Verarmte, Beraubte
dennoch leben
planen bauen
so vieles.